CHECK-IN CHECK-OUT

CHECK-IN CHECK-OUT

SUVRADEEP GAURANGA GHOSH
Faculty Member (Front Office Department)
J.P. Institute of Hotel Management and Catering Technology
Meerut (Uttar Pradesh)

AMAN PUBLICATIONS
NEW DELHI

Published by
Rajiv Jain for Aman Publications
LG-4A, Ganpati Bhawan,
4675-B/21, Ansari Road,
Darya Ganj, Delhi - 110002
PH: 23255012, 23282127
E-mail: sshjbs@yahoo.com

Reprint **2020**

ISBN–81–8204–027–2

SOLE DISTRIBUTOR
JINDAL BOOK SERVICES
LG-4A, Ganpati Bhawan,
4675-B/21, Ansari Road,
Darya Ganj, Delhi - 110002

Jacket Designed by :
S.M. Graphics

Printed by:
NCT Printers & Publishers, Delhi, India

Preface

The book is a comprehensive effort to make the hospitality program educators, career guidance counselors, aspiring young students passing out from their alma mater, young hotel management professionals to have a sound theoretical and practical knowledge about the various dimensions of front office operations and management in the modern hotel industry in the world of hospitality.

The book has a detailed coverage of the major activities of front office department of the hotels and thus encompasses the various functions of the Front Office performed during the entire guest cycle which includes processing reservation, registering the guest on arrival, providing various services to the guest during their occupancy and processing the settlement of their bills during departure.

The book has stated the importance of Front Office as a major line function and operational department in bringing valuable revenue to the hotel by the challenging task of selling the "rooms" which are products as the revenue of a particular unsold room lost for one day can never be recovered for that particular day.

The book also has a brief coverage of the management function of Front Office in evaluating the degree to which the aims and objectives of a particular hotel organization is achieved and also the rate at which an organization is progressing towards its established periodic goals set and thus functioning in accordance with the mission and vision of an organization at large.

The book also has tried to enhance the personal and practical skills of the aspiring professionals by providing them a brief knowledge about inculcation of various qualities required to become a successful hotel management professional.

Thus, the book has been written and compiled with great efforts to develop all the qualities, traits and knowledge in a professional required by the leading hospitality companies around the country in order to flourish in the field of hospitality as an asset for the various hospitality organizations.

SUVRADEEP G. GHOSH

Faculty Member (Front Office Department)
J.P. Institute of Hotel Management
and Catering Technology
Meerut (Uttar Pradesh)

Acknowledgements

I express my sincere gratitude and thanks to the following intellectuals under whose guidance the entire concept of writing and compiling this book have been developed: -

1. **Mr. Anil Pramod Rastogi**, (Director, J.P. Institute of Hotel Management and Catering Technology) for his guidance and help in conceiving the entire idea of literature of the book.

2. **Mr. D.S. Negi** (Senior Faculty Member, Department of Hotel Management: Rohilkhand University, Barielly, Uttar Pradesh)

3. **Mr. Rupesh Srivastava** (Senior Faculty Member, Banarasidas Insitute of Hotel Management: Lucknow, Uttar Pradesh)

SUVRADEEP G. GHOSH

Faculty Member (Front Office Department)
J.P. Institute of Hotel Management
and Catering Technology
Meerut (Uttar Pradesh)

About the Author

The author is an emerging name in the field of hospitality literature. He has been a meritorious student throughout his life and has joined the field of hospitality academics as a young aspiring academician with the ability to give his best with his hard work, analytical capacity and a strong motive of giving the Indian hotel management students a book which can prepare them for specialization in Front Office for the various interviews which they are going to face for entering in the hospitality industry and thus make a successful career. With this view he developed his first work in the year 2005 "*Front Office Training Manual*" which was a huge success.

The present book is the second work in the field of hotel front office which also promises to maintain the same standard of success.

The author completed his

1. **Master's Degree in Tourism Management** from the Indira Gandhi National Open University, Delhi. (2006)
2. **Bachelor's Degree in Hospitality Management** from the Robert Gordon University, Aberdeen, Scotland through the Institute of Advanced Management, Salt Lake, Kolkata. (2002)
3. **Diploma in Hotel Management and Catering Technology** from the Institute of Advanced Management, Salt Lake, Kolkata. (2002)
4. **Diploma in Hospitality Management** from the Educational Institute of the American and Lodging

Association (AH&LA). (2002)

The authorization was the recipient of Gold Medal for securing the 1st rank in the Degree Program and also got several awards including a medal for scoring the highest marks in Front Office in the Diploma Examination.

The author is presently working as a **faculty member in Front Office department in J.P. Institute of Hotel Management and Catering Technology**, Meerut, Uttar Pradesh.

Contents

Preface *v*

Acknowledgements *vii*

About the Author *ix*

1. Introduction to Tourism, Hospitality and Hotel Industry **1-6**

- Tourism and its Importance 1
- Hospitality and its Origin 2
- Hotels, their Evolution and Growth 4

2. Organization **7-19**

- The Various Sections of Front Office 7
- Duties and Responsibilities of Front Office Personnel 10
- Attributes of a Front Office Personnel 18

3. Types of Rooms **20-23**

- Some Special Room Types and Categories and their Abbreviations 20
- Meal Plans Used in the Hotel Industry 23

4. Hotel Entrance, Lobby and Front Office **24-34**

- The Layout of Front Office 24
- Front Office Equipment 27

5. Reservation **35-49**

- Importance of Reservation 35
- Modes of Reservation 36
- Channels or Sources of Reservation 37

- Types of Reservation 39
- Systems of Reservation 42
- Cancellations, Amendments and Overbooking 46

6. **Registration** **50-63**
   - The Six Steps of the Registration Process 50
   - Pre-registration Activity 51
   - Creation of the Registration Record 52
   - Assignment of the Room and Rate 53
   - Establishment of the Method of Payment 55
   - Issual of the Room Key 58
   - Fulfillment of Special Requests 59
   - When Guests Cannot be Accommodated 61
7. **Front Office Coordination** **64-67**
   - Interdepartmental Coordination of Front Office with Other Departments 64
8. **On-going Responsibilities** **68-78**
   - Communication within Front Office 68
   - Guest Services 72
   - Guest Relations and Complaint Handling 74
9. **During The Stay Activities** **79-88**
   - Information Services 79
   - Guest Room Key Control 81
   - Messages and Mail Handling 82
   - Hospitality Desk 84
   - Complaints Handling 85
   - Guest History 87
10. **Room Selling Techniques** **89-92**
    - Upselling at the Front Desk 89
    - Discounts 90

11.	**Night Audit in Front Office**	**93-105**
	• Night Audit in Front Office	93
	• The Night Audit and its Main Functions	95
	• Details of The Night Audit Process	96
	• The Ten Steps of Night Audit	96
	• The Various Types of Errors in the Night Audit	103
12.	**Hospitality**	**106-116**
	• Hospitality and its Delivery	106
	• Service Management	109
13.	**Computers in Hospitality**	**117-125**
	• Computers in Hospitality	117
Bibliography		127-130

1

INTRODUCTION TO TOURISM, HOSPITALITY AND HOTEL INDUSTRY

TOURISM AND ITS IMPORTANCE

Definition

Tourism can be defined as travel of people from their place of residence to a particular destination for the purpose of leisure, business, pilgrimage, visiting friends and relatives and other important activities.

Contribution of Tourism to a Particular Destination

- Tourism is a very important economic activity and helps in the overall development of a particular destination.
- Realizing the importance of tourism, most of the developed and developing countries of the world have started granting tourism a status of a full-fledged industry.
- The following are the major contributions of tourism to a particular destination: -

1. Generation of Employment

- Tourism helps in the generation of employment to the local people in a large number of industries producing tourism products and services for the tourists.
- Thus, employment opportunities are generated in the hospitality industry, travel industry and other supporting industries.

2. Generation of Foreign Exchange

- Tourism helps to attract large number foreign tourists to a particular tourist destination.
- Thus, tourism helps to earn a good amount of foreign currency for a tourist destination and thus improves the economic condition of the tourist destination.

3. Improvement of Infrastructure

- The tourism also helps in the improvement of the basic infra-structure of a particular destination such as roads, electricity, water supply, sewage and public transportation system.
- This helps to bring about an overall improvement and development of a tourist destination and also encourages the growth of other industries.

4. Socio-cultural Upliftment

- Tourism also helps to promote the culture of the local people destination and gives them international exposure.
- Tourism helps to improve social standards of the local people of the tourist destination.

HOSPITALITY AND ITS ORIGIN

The word ***"Hospitality"*** means a friendly treatment, which is offered to a stranger. The concept of Hospitality has diversified to a huge extent after the process of globalization, which has taken place in most of the countries of the earth.

The Travel and Tourism Industry is perhaps one of the largest and fastest growing industries in the whole world due to the increase in the inflow of tourists in the various countries due to increase in business between the nations, increasing spending power of the people, curiosity to visit new countries and learn new culture and improvement in the means of communication.

The Travel and Tourism Industry has many dimensions such as Hospitality Industry, Transportation Services and the Events and Activities.

The **Hospitality Industry** is broadly classified into: -

- The **Lodging Industry** that includes hotels, motels, casinos, resorts, parks, hostels and other type of accommodation.
- The **Foodservice Industry** that includes restaurants, fast food counters, kiosks, bars, tea and coffee houses, snack bars, institutional food service catering and so on.

In ancient times, most of the travellers were either traders in search of markets or were warriors for capturing new territories and there were no organized forms of accommodation.

Inn keeping can be said to be the first commercial enterprise and hospitality was one of the first service for which money was exchanged.

In ancient times, the inns were communal rooms offering accommodation at reasonable rates, but did not have any sanitation facilities.

In the 3rd century AD, the Roman empire developed an extensive network of roads throughout Europe and Asia and a chain of roadside lodges was constructed and along the major route from Spain to Turkey.

Till the Industrial Revolution of the 1700s, no significant improvement was made in the inns and taverns and they were not very suitable for wealthy travellers and so special commercial establishments called "*Hotels*" were constructed for providing lodging and foodservices to them.

Thus, the origin of the word hospitality has an ancient history and so, the hospitality industry is considered as one of the most ancient industries of the world.

HOTELS, THEIR EVOLUTION AND GROWTH

The lodging industry is perhaps the oldest commercial industry of the world and is a fast growing industry with a lot of career opportunities.

The establishment of money during the sixth century B.C. gave the opportunity to the people to trade and travel. Thus, the origin of hotel can be traced back to the sixth century B.C which was in the form of inns which were the first type of hotels to cater to the lodging requirements of the travellers. These inns were managed by the husband and wife team who provided the travellers with overnight accommodation by allowing the travellers to sleep on the floor and make their own beds. They also provided food and wines and some other types of facilities. Thus, the entire services were provided by the husband and wife teams along with some type of recreation facilities such as music, dance and some types of indoor games.

The beginning of industrial revolution in Europe introduced the new idea in the business of inn-keeping as traveling become more frequent after the development of other means of transportation such as the railways and ships. The industrial revolution also gave a rise to a new dimension of travel known as the business in which people started traveling one from place to another for their purpose of business.

In England, in earlier days, public houses called ***"Inns"*** were constructed for the noble and elite class of guests. At the same time low and mid-budget properties called ***"Taverns"*** were also constructed for catering to the needs of the common people.

In France, finer lodging establishments called ***"Hotelleries"*** were constructed to cater to the needs of the rich and noble class of people while "cabarets" were constructed for catering to the needs of the common people.

Similarly other native form of hostelry also became popular in other parts of the world such as ***"Riokan"*** in Japan, ***"Paradors"*** in Spain and ***"Pousadas"*** in Portugal.

England was the first country to use the term ***"Hotel"*** to these commercial lodging establishments in the year 1760 A.D. In the United States of America, the lodging establishments were called ***"Inns"*** of ***"Coffee Houses"***.

U.S.A was the first country where the real growth of hotels took place when the first building for hotel purposes was built in the year 1794 called the "City Hotel" in New York. This was followed by an era of competition in the field of the hotel industry as many beautiful hotels were constructed at this time.

The concept of the operation of the chain hotel was introduced in the field of the hotel industry with the beginning of the first commercial hotel by Ellsworth Statler in 1908 A.D. called ***"The Buffalo Statler"***.

In 1930, there was a Great Economic Depression in United States and Europe which sank the business of the hotel industry into an all time low. The effects of the Depression in United States were so severe that about 85% of the hotels in United States went either into receivership or through some form of liquidation.

After the Great Economic Depression which hit the lodging industry very badly in United States, there was a speedy recovery in this industry during and after the World War II.

Landmarks in The History of The Hotel Industry

YEAR	EVENT
1794 A.D.	The first commercial building for the hotel purposes called "The City Hotel" was constructed in New York, U.S.A.
1829 A.D.	The "Tremont House", first class hotel was constructed in Boston, U.S.A.
1875 A.D	The most expensive hotel of its day called "The Palace" was built in San Francisco.
1908 A.D.	Ellsworth started the first commercial hotels called "The Buffalo Chain of Hotels".
1915 A.D.	The international chains of hotels were started.
1930 A.D.	The Economic Depression led to the decline of the hotel industry.
1939 A.D. - 1945 A.D.	There was an increase in the number of hotels during World War II.

2

ORGANIZATION

THE VARIOUS SECTIONS OF FRONT OFFICE

Reservation

- The reservation section is a very important section of front office as this section deals with the important job of booking rooms for the free individual traveler guests as well as groups.
- The staffs of the reservation department take bookings from the guest through various ways such as letters, fax, telephones as well as e-mail.
- The staffs of the reservation department maintain accurate room inventory information and also maintain an up-to-date inventory list of the available rooms for the various dates.
- The reservation staffs also take various group bookings such as airline crew bookings as well as other corporate group bookings and thus earn valuable revenue for the hotel.

Reception or Registration

- The reception or the registration department is one of the most important section of the front office as this staff of this section remain indirect contact with the guest right from the time of their arrival till their time of departure.

- The reception staffs welcome the guests on their arrival at the hotel and register them in the hotel and assign guestrooms to the guests in the hotel.
- The reception staffs assign rooms to guests coming with reservations as well as guests coming without reservation.
- The reception staffs also deal with the various problems of the guests during their stay at the hotel.
- Thus the reception staff maintain a thorough guest contact during the stay of the guest at the hotel in order to ensure that the guest do not face any sort of problems during their say at the hotel.

Cash

- The cash section of the front office also plays an important role as these sections maintain the various accounts of the guest during their stay at the hotel.
- The cash section of the front office ensures that all the expenditure incurred by the guests during their stay at the hotel are properly recorded in the accounts of the guests.
- The cash section also ensures that the various accounts of the guest are accurate and complete regularly by the process of night.
- The cash section also prepares various reports such as daily operations report, occupancy report as well as manager's report and various other reports important from the point of management.

Bell Desk

- The bell desk is also an important department which is generally included as a section in the front office of the hotel.

- This is also a very important section of the front office as the bell attendants are the first staff s with whom the guests are in contact the moment the entire the lobby of the hotel.
- The bell attendants help the guests to help them in the transportation of the luggage from the lobby to the guestrooms as well as from the guestrooms to the lobby during the arrival and departure of the guests.
- The bell attendants also perform various other important duties such as supplying magazines and newspapers to the guestrooms as well as paging the names of the guests on paging boards in the lobby as well as in other public areas.
- The bell attendants also sell stamps to the guests on demand as well as do various jobs for the guests within the hotels as well as outside of the hotel on request.

Telephone Exchange

- The telephone exchange is also a very important section of the front office as it performs the important job of directing the various incoming as well as outgoing telephone calls of the hotel.
- The telephone exchange staffs also compile the bills of the guests incurring various STD as well as ISD call charges.
- The telephone exchange also performs the very important function placing the various wake-up calls for the guests on request.

Information

- The information section is also an important part of the front office as this section plays an important role in providing valuable information to the guests regarding the hotel, city and the country at large.

- The information sections has a concierge as it is important staff whose main duty is to provide information regarding various travel related as well as other types of information to the guests as well as booking tickets for the guests in various concerts as well as various other events going around in the city.

DUTIES AND RESPONSIBILITIES OF FRONT OFFICE PERSONNEL

Job Description of Front Office Manager

Job Position Title	:	FRONT OFFICE MANAGER
Job Category	:	Managerial
Reports To	:	General Manager
Position Summary	:	Directly supervises and manages all the front office staff and ensures the proper completion of all the activities of the front office. Co-ordinates interdepartmentally as well as interdepartmentally with in the hotels for the proper achievement of the goals and mission of the hotel.
Hours of Operation	:	Eight hour shift each day or according to the policy of the hotel management.

Duties and Responsibilities:

(1) Actively participates in the recruitment and selection of the front office personnel.

(2) Prepares the working schedules of the front office supervisors and other executives with in the department.

(3) Supervises the working of the executives as well as other staff in each shift.

(4) Keeps an accurate track of the amount of contribution of the front office department in the total business of the hotel.

(5) Prepares monthly and annual forecasts of the total revenue to be generated by the front office from the sale of rooms.

(6) Operates the front office department within the allotted budget for the department.

(7) Resolves all the guest complaints and problems effectively and follow ups the same.

Educational Qualification : Four years Degree or Three years Diploma in Hotel Management and Catering Technology from a recognized university or an institute.

Experience : Minimum five years of hotel experience with two years experience as a front office supervisor.

Job Description of Lobby Manager/Guest Relation Executive

Job Position Title : LOBBY MANAGER / GUEST RELATION EXECUTIVE

Job Category : Managerial

Reports To : Front Office Manager or General Manager

Position Summary : Supervises the overall functio-ning of the various sections of the front office including reception, reservation, bell desk and telephone exchange.

Hours of Operation : Eight hour shift each day or according to the policy of the hotel management.

Duties and Responsibilities:

1) Takes the attendance of the front office staff and checks their grooming at the beginning of each shift.
2) Trains the various staff of the front office in providing guest service.
3) Welcomes the VIP guests with garlands and offering welcome drinks on their arrival.
4) He maintains a detailed knowledge of the room status and reservation status and answers the various e-mails and letters of queries from the guest.
5) He also keeps a detailed knowledge of the various services and facilities available in the hotel so as to inform the guests about the same.
6) He anticipates the various incidents of guest dissatisfaction and tries to solve the problems of the guests within the policy laid down by the hotel management.

Educational Qualification : Four years Degree or Three years Diploma in Hotel Management and Catering Technology from a reputed and affiliated university or college.

Experience : Minimum two years of hotel experience with one year experience as a front office supervisor.

Job Description of Front Desk Assistant

Job Position Title : FRONT DESK ASSISTANT

Job Category : Non-supervisory

Reports To : Lobby Manager or Front Office Manager

Position Summary : Registers and assigns rooms to the guests on their arrival, represents the front office ad remains in direct contact with the guests throughout the guest cycle.

Hours of Operation : Eight hour shift each day or according to the policy of the hotel management.

Duties and Responsibilities:

1) Possesses a thorough knowledge about handling guests and should have all the basic etiquettes while handling the guests especially through telephones..
2) Possesses a thorough knowledge about the rooms of the hotel that includes the room location, types, plans and rates applicable.
3) Maintains an update room status information which includes the number of occupied rooms in the hotel, number of out of order rooms in the hotel, number of vacànt rooms in the hotel and so on.
4) Possess a thorough knowledge about handling the various front office equipment such as the telephone and computers.
5) Uses proper mail, message and parcel handling procedures.
6) Processes guest check-out during the last stage of the guest cycle which is departure.

Educational Qualification : Graduate from any stream from a recognized college or an university or Three years Diploma in Hotel Management and Catering Technology from a reputed and affiliated university or college.

Experience : Previous hotel experience desired but not compulsory.

JOB DESCRIPTION OF RESERVATION ASSISTANT

Job Position Title : RESERVATION ASSISTANT

Job Category : Non-supervisory

Reports To : Lobby Manager or Front Office Manager

Position Summary : Processes the reservation of the guests through the central reservation system or any other sources of reservation and handles the various queries of the guests regarding reservation.

Hours of Operation : Eight hour shift each day or according to the policy of the hotel management.

Duties and Responsibilities:

1) Receives and handles the various reservation enquiries through telephone, telex, fax, e-mail and other modes of communication.
2) Receive reservation from the sales and marketing division of the hotel property.
3) Possesses a thorough knowledge and information about the types and availability of rooms of the hotel property.
4) Possesses detailed information about the various

rules and regulations of the hotel while processing the reservation requests of the guests.

5) Possesses total information about the various plans, packages and discounts to be offered to the guests during the process of reservation.

6) Communicates the confirmed reservations to the front desk.

Educational Qualification : Four years Degree or Three years Diploma in Hotel Management and Catering Technology from a reputed and affiliated university or college. Command in reading , writing and speaking English and preferably knowledge of a foreign language.

Experience : Minimum two years of hotel experience with one year experience as a front office supervisor.

JOB DESCRIPTION OF BELL CAPTAIN

Job Position Title : BELL CAPTAIN

Job Category : Supervisory

Reports To : Lobby Manager

Position Summary : To supervise and inspect the overall activities of the bell boys in providing efficient guest services.

Hours of Operation : Eight hour shift each day or according to the policy of the hotel management.

Duties and Responsibilities:

1) Records the attendance of the bellboys at the beginning of each shift and to brief them about their activities and conduct during the shift.
2) Ensures that all the bellboys are properly groomed and geared up for providing the guest service.
3) Controls the movement of the bellboys by maintaining the lobby control sheet which is a summary of the activities of all the bellboys.
4) Maintains the left luggage register to keep a record of all the luggage of the various guests those have been kept at the bell desk.
5) Maintains the scanty baggage register for keeping a record of all the guests who have arrived at the hotel property with a very few luggage.
6) Arranges for paging service for the guests within the hotel property as and when required.
7) Supervises the crew and group wake-up call procedure.

Educational Qualification : Graduation from any stream from a recognized college or university or One-year post graduate Diploma in Hotel Management and Catering Technology.

Experience : Minimum two years of hotel experience as a bellboy.

JOB DESCRIPTION OF BELL BOY

Job Position Title : BELL BOY

Job Category : Non-supervisory

Reports To : Bell Captain or Lobby Manager

Position Summary : Provides transportation services, paging services and other errands assigned by the guests.

Hours of Operation : Eight hour shift each day or according to the policy of the hotel management.

Duties and Responsibilities:

1) Transports the luggage of the guest from the porch to the lobby of the hotel during the arrival of the guest.
2) Transports the luggage of the guest from the lobby to the guestroom of the guest after the process of registration.
3) To bring down the luggage of the guest from the guestroom to the lobby area at the time of the departure of the guest.
4) Delivers newspapers, magazines, máils and other messages of the guest to the guestrooms.
5) Pages guests in the lobby area, restaurants and other public area within the hotel property.
6) Properly keeps the luggage of the guests in the left luggage room on request and issue luggage tags to the guest.
7) Keep a track of all the scanty baggage guests to the bell captain.

Educational Qualification : Graduation from any stream from a recognized college or university or One-year appren-ticeship programme in bell desk and front office procedure.

Experience : No preliminary experience is required.

ATTRIBUTES OF A FRONT OFFICE PERSONNEL

A High Sense of Personal Grooming:

1. Uniforms must be clean and neatly pressed.
2. Hairs should be well groomed.
3. Nails should be properly trimmed
4. It is essential to take a bath regularly and preferably soft cologne should be used.
5. Jewellery should be restricted for the ladies.

A High Sense of Personal Hygiene:

1. A clean appearance of the front office personnel is essential for the proper projection of good image of the hotel in front of the hotel.

Self Confidence:

1. It is extremely essential that a front office personnel should have the self confidence to meet the guests coming from different countries and different culture and language and make them feel comfortable in the hotel.

Communication Must be Clear and Correct:

1. It is always preferable that the front office personnel should know more than one language and specially a foreign language to communicate with the foreigner guests.

Diplomacy:

1. It is again an essential quality of the front office personnel to have a diplomatic approach towards the guests in order to diffuse any type of tension, which may occur due to the poor service of the hotel.

A Good Memory:

1. It is rare attribute present in very few of the front staffs and this ability differentiates the good front

office staff from the average because the guests feel extremely happy if they are being addressed by their names.

Good Manners:

1. This is supposed to be the basic quality that should be present in all the staffs of the hospitality industry.
2. Good manners are the essence of hospitality and will thus attract more guests and will thus maintain the good will of the hotel and the industry at large.

Physical Fitness:

1. Front office operations require that the front office personnel should be physically fit and active so that they are able to serve the guest with smile and pleasure.

Quick Decision Making Ability:

1. The front office staff should have the ability to improvise and solve the various problems of the guests requiring quick decision making ability and at the same time take care that the interest of the organization is not at stake.

3

TYPES OF ROOMS

SOME SPECIAL ROOM TYPES AND CATEGORIES AND THEIR ABBREVIATIONS

Single Room (SGL or S)	:	A Single room is a room which has a single bed. this type of room is normally assigned to one person.
Double Room (DBL or D)	:	A Double room is a room which has a double or a composite bed. This type of room is normally assigned to two persons.
Triple Room	:	A Triple Room is a room which is assigned to three persons. It may have two or more beds.
Quad Room	:	A Quad room is a room which is assigned to four persons. It may have two or more beds.
King Room (K)	:	A King Room is a room with a king-size bed. It may be occupied by one or more persons.

Queen Room (Q) : A queen Room is a room with a queen-size bed. It may be occupied by one or more persons.

Twin Room (T) : A Twin room is a room which has two single beds. This type of room is also normally assigned to two persons.

Twin Double Room : This is a room which has two double beds beds separated from each other. This type of room is normally assigned to four persons. these rooms are normally assigned to families and are therefore called Family Room.

Hollywood Twin Bed Room : This is a room which has two single beds with a single head board common for both.

Parlor : A Parlor is a sitting or a living room and generally not used as a bedroom.

Studio Room : A Studio room is a parlor with a studio bed or a couch. *(A bed which can be converted into a sofa during the day.)*

Suite Room : A Suite room consists of a parlor with connected with one or more bedrooms.

Junior Suite Room : A Junior Suite room is a large room with a Partition separating the living room from the bedroom.

Duplex : A duplex is a set of rooms not situated on the level and connected by a staircase. Generally The parlor is at the lower level and the bedroom is at the upper level.

Efficiency Room : A room that has some sort of kitchen facilities attached to it is called an Efficiency Room. these type of rooms are usually found in resorts and residential hotels.

Hospitality Room : A Hospitality Room is a room which is used by a guest to entertain his own guests and usually charged on an hourly basis.

Penthouse Suite : A Penthouse Suite is a set of rooms situated on on the terrace level part of which may be opened to the sky.

Adjoining Rooms : Adjoining Rooms are two or more rooms having a common wall but no connecting door in between.

Interconnecting Rooms : Interconnecting Rooms are two or more rooms with private connecting doors permitting access between rooms without having to go into the corridor.

Adjacent Rooms : These are guestrooms near to each other and located across the corridor.

Cabana : A Cabana is a room adjacent to the swimming pool area with or without sleeping facility and have generally facilities to change and having light showers.

Lanai : A Lanai is a room with a good view. It generally has a balcony overlooking the garden or the swimming pool. These are generally found in resort hotels.

MEAL PLANS USED IN THE HOTEL INDUSTRY

EUROPEAN PLAN (E P) : Room charge + Early Morning Tea.

CONTINENTAL PLAN (C P) : Room charge + Early Morning Tea + Continental Breakfast.

AMERICAN PLAN (A P) : Room charge + Early Morning Tea + Breakfast + Lunch + High Tea + Dinner. This plan is also called the *Full Board Plan* or *Full Pension*.

MODIFIED AMERICAN (MAP) : Room charge + Early Morning Tea + **PLAN** Breakfast/ High Tea + Lunch\Dinner. This plan is also called the *Half Board Plan* or *Semi Pension*

BERMUDA PLAN (B P) : Room Charges + Early Morn-ing Tea + American Break-fast.

4

HOTEL ENTRANCE, LOBBY AND FRONT OFFICE

THE LAYOUT OF FRONT OFFICE

The Concept of Hotel Entrance

- The main entrance of the hotel plays a very important role in creating a right image in the minds of the guests and thus helps them in the selection of the hotel.
- The main entrance should be identifiable and should be able to direct the guests to the lobby of the hotel.
- The main entrance should be spacious enough to accommodate the guests coming to the hotel through cars and taxis.
- Generally, according to the rule, the driveway in front of the porch of the hotel should be at least 18 feet wide in order to accommodate at least two cars or light vehicles.
- The hotel entrance should have an optimum number of steps to lead to the lobby in order to give the lobby area and elevated appearance.

- There should be a separate entrance from the driveway to the lobby in the form of a ramp.

The Concept of Hotel Lobby

- The lobby is the general waiting area of the hotel and includes sitting arrangements for the patrons, guests and visitors.
- The entire front office department is situated in the lobby of the hotel and an official called the Lobby Manager controls the area.
- A large number of sections of front office are situated in the lobby area such as bell desk, cash, information, reception, lobby and travel desk.
- Various restaurants, food and beverage outlets, gift shops and even banquet halls are situated in the lobby area of the hotel.

DIFFERENCE BETWEEB THE TERM "FRONT OFFICE" AND "RECEPTION"

The Front Office

- The term "***Front Office***" is best explained by reference to the physical layout of hotels of varying size.
- In a world class hotel, it may be seen that a large number of departments grouped around the foyer area of the hotel to deal with the guests not only on arrival and departure but also throughout their stay.
- Because they are situated in the ***foyer area***, which is easily accessible to the guests, for convenience they are grouped together under the term "***Front Office***".

The Reception Desk

- The "***Reception Desk***" is one small part of the total front office and therefore in a world-class type and size of hotel, forms a single department within the complete front office.
- But in small hotels with less strength of staffs, there may be only one or two staffs in this department dealing with the guests during their arrival, departure and stay. So, it will be wise to group them under the term "***Reception***".

Layout of The Reception Desk or the Front Desk

- While deciding upon the basic design aspects of the reception desk or the front desk, it is important to consider the following parameters: -

1. Size

- The sizes of the front desk or reception are small in fully automated hotels where there are computers and have less mechanical equipments.
- But in hotels having no computers, the sizes of the front desks or the reception desks are big in order to accommodate a large number of mechanical equipments.

2. Shape

- The shape of the front desk should match the shape of the lobby and should fit well in the lobby.
- E.g. Circular shape (*Circular lobby*), L-shape (*L lobby*), Straight shape (*Straight lobby*), Curve shape

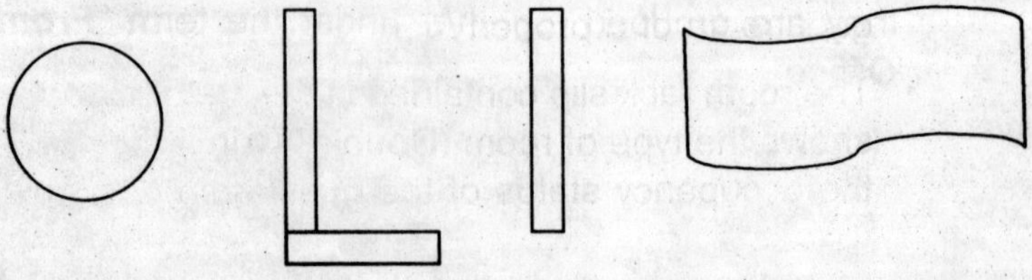

FRONT OFFICE EQUIPMENT

Equipments Used in Front Office

- A large number of factors play a very important role in the choice of equipments to kept or installed in the front office of a hotel to carry out the day to day administration and management of the department.
- The factors include the system of operations prevailing in front office, the size of the hotel, the level of automation and the budget of the hotel.
- A big hotel having a high budget will definitely choose an automated front office with fully automated or computerized equipments.
- A big hotel having limited budget will opt for a semi-automated front office with semi-automated equipments.
- A small hotel with limited budget will choose a non-automated system of front office operations with non-automated front office equipments.

List of Manual Equipments Used in Front Office Operations

1. Room Rack

- The room rack is a large front office equipment located just behind the front desk.
- The room rack is a wooden framework designed and contains a metallic array of pockets which contain a large number of room rack slips for showing the reservation and housekeeping status of each guestroom of a property.
- The room rack slip contained in the metallic pockets shows the type of room (Double, Twin, King, Suite), the occupancy status of the guestroom (Occupied,

Vacant, Not Cleared) and the name of the guest registered in the guestroom.

- The current occupancy status of the guestrooms is indicated by the colored strips inserted in the pockets of the room rack.
- It is the joint effort of the front desk and housekeeping to timely update the room rack in order to have an accurate room status position.

2. Information Rack

- The information rack is another important devise positioned in the front desk and is used by the front desk agent to track the various in-house guests of the hotel.
- The information is a revolving devise that contains information about the various guests presently registered in the hotel with the name of the guests alphabetically arranged in the rack and the information taken from the upper portion of the folios of the guests.
- The information contained in the information rack are name of the guest, number and type of room occupied, rate of the guestroom, date of arrival and departure and the billing instructions.

3. Mail and Message Rack

- The mail and message rack is a wooden framework containing an array of pigeonholes with each pigeonhole used to store the various mails and messages received for an in-house guest.
- Previously, the mail and message rack used to contain the keys of the guestrooms in the pigeonholes and was thus called the mail, message and key rack.

- But nowadays, the mail rack has been isolated from the key rack and has been moved behind scenes to present a more professional appearance and at the same time ensuring the security of the mails and messages of the guests of the hotel.

4. Key Rack or Key Drawer

- The key rack or the key drawer is an important front office equipment located underneath the counter of the front desk.
- The key rack as the name suggests, is a wooden or metallic framework containing an array of slots used for keeping the keys of the guestrooms in sequential order of the guestrooms present in the hotel.
- This rack is maintained by the front desk in hotels where metal or hard keys are used and is thus an essential front desk equipment for such hotels.

5. Folio Well or Folio Bucket

- A folio well or folio bucket is also an important equipment used in the front desk cash section.
- This equipment contains a large number of slots where the folios are arranged sequentially according to the room number.
- The folio well is used by the front office cashier to store and track the folios of the various registered guests of the hotel and is used to maintain the folios safely for future use and reference.

List of Semi-automated Equipments Used in Front Office Operations

1. Posting Machine

- The accounting posting machine is a very essential equipment used in the semi-automated front office system for posting the various charges in the accounts of the guests.

- The posting machine is generally used to calculate the totals of the guest accounts, departments and transactions.
- The mechanical features of the accounting posting machine are arranged in such a logical sequence the job of posting the charges into the various guest accounts becomes very easy.
- The line pick-up keys ensures that the posting machine is not over printing a line as the operator indicates where the accounting posting machine should start the calculation and should start printing.
- There is a key pad in the account posting machine which is used by the cashier or the operator to enter the room numbers of the guests, department key (*e.g. room, tax, food*) and also the type of transaction (*e.g. debit, credit, transfer*)

2. Cash Register

- The cash register is an semi-automated equipment used optionally by the front desk.
- The cash register is generally used by the front desk to record the various sales of sundries at the front desk such as stamps, newspapers, candy etc.
- The various required mechanical features present in the cash register include a key pad, category key (*stamps, newspapers, candy*) and amount entering key.

3.Wake-up Devices

- The wake-up device is a very important device used by the front desk or the telephone exchange of non-automated or semi-automated hotels to remind the staffs of awakening the guests at requested times.

- The most famous and common wake-up device is known as the James Remindo Timer which is an alarm clock with pull-out pins.
- Many hotels also use a simple alarm clock for awakening the guests. The guests' requests for wake-up calls are recorded in a wake-up sheet with the information of time, room number and name of the guest.
- In fully automated systems, the telephone exchange automatically places the various requests of the guests for wake-up calls by automatic-voice-recorded wake-up messages. This feature is of great help when many guests have to be woken up at the same time in the hotel.

4. Credit Card Imprinter

- The credit card imprinter is a very important equipment used for the purpose of front office accounting.
- This equipment is used especially when the guests present credit cards at the time of their arrival or departure to settle their bill.
- The credit card imprinter makes an imprint of the credit card used by the guest as a method of payment.

5. Typewriter

- The typewriter is very important semi-automated equipment used for preparing various documents related to the front office operations and also related to the guests.
- The front office employees use typewriters to prepare guest reservation confirmation letter, to prepare the

registration card of the guest and also to conduct the other word processing jobs of the department.

List of Automated Equipments Used in Front Office Operations

1. Credit Card Validator

- The credit card validator is automated front office equipment used by the front office cashier to check the validity of the credit card presented by the guest as a mode of payment at the time of arrival or departure of the guest.
- This equipment is a computer terminal linked to a credit card data bank, which holds information concerning the validity of the credit card of the guest.
- The credit card equipment assures the hotel management that the guest has credit balance high enough to cover the projected charges and it also verifies that the card presented by the guest is not a stolen property.

2. Time Stamping Machine

- The time stamping is a mechanical or an electronic device which is used extensively by the front office of a hotel record the check-in and check-out time of the guests, delivery time of any mail or message for the in-house guests.
- This device imprints the date and time on a piece of paper either electronically or mechanically and is thus an important equipment for carrying out the operations of the front office leading to guest satisfaction.

3. Fax Machines

- The full form of FAX machine is Facsimile Automated Xerox machine and is an important electronic equipment used in the front desk for communication purposes.

- This is a facsimile reproduction equipment that operates through telephone lines and are used extensively by the front office to receive and send official documents important from the point of view of the guest or the hotel management at large.
- While sending a fax message, the operator dials the destination fax machine number and then sends the fax message by inserting the message page in the machine.
- It is important that the destination fax machine should be switched on when the fax message is sent from the hotel.

4. *Call Accounting System*

- A call accounting system is a fully computerized telephone system which allows the proper billings of the outgoing calls of the guests.
- This type of automated telephone system has been introduced in a large number of hotels nowadays due to the reason for providing improved services to the guest.
- The call accounting system is called APBX or the Automated Private Branch Exchange and is used in the hotel telephone exchange section of the front office department to automatically trace and bill the outgoing calls made by the guests during their stay at the hotel.

5. *Computer*

- All the automated hotels around the world are excessively using computers for the day to day operations, administration and management.

- Computers are also used widely in the front office departments of the hotels for the purpose of reservation, registration, accounting and auditing.
- Computers are efficient to operate and are extremely user friendly and thus help the employees to store and retrieve important data of the guest from time to time to carry out the various guest services.

5

RESERVATION

IMPORTANCE OF RESERVATION

- The reservation section is a vital part of the front office department of a hotel and it plays an important role in the sale of guestrooms by taking future room bookings and thus plays an important role in generation of revenue for the hotel.
- The following are the main functions of the reservation section of a hotel: -
  1. Receiving the reservation request from the guest
  2. Checking the room availability for accepting the reservation request
  3. To process the reservation request either for accepting or denying the same
  4. Communicating the reservation confirmation to the guests and keeping a record of the same.
  5. Processing reservation modifications and cancellations according to the request of the guests and also according to the availability of guestrooms.
  6. *Ensuring full occupancy of the guestrooms of the hotel by taking future reservations.*

- The reservation section gives the hotel a chance to equate the guest inquiry with the rooms' availability and thus, gives the hotel sufficient time to arrange and prepare for the most suitable accommodation for the guests.
- The section also forecasts and gives good indication of the level of business that the hotel might get in future.
- Thus, to a great extent the hotel can forecast the future revenue generation keeping in mind the reservation business.
- The reservation section also helps the hotel in scheduling and reorganizing the staff the front office and other departments might need for the future period.
- The reservation section also helps the hotel to equate the needs of the guest with the available product.
- Thus, the main importance of the reservation section is that it sells the main perishable product of the hotel i.e. room and increase the chance of revenue earning for the hotel.

MODES OF RESERVATION

VERBAL	WRITTEN
e.g. Telephone	e.g. Letter Telex Fax E-mail

VERBAL MODES

The following are the verbal modes in which a reservation request reaches a hotel: -

Telephone:

- Prospective guests may telephone the hotel directly.
- This is the most common method of direct reservation communications.

WRITTEN MODES

The following are the written modes in which a reservation request reaches a hotel: -

Mail:

- Written requests for reservations are common for group, tour, and convention business.
- Generally, mail requests are sent directly to the reservation department of the destination property.

Telex, Cable, Fax, E-mail and Other:

- Telex is often used to communicate the international reservation requests.
- Cable, fax and other methods of communication account for a small proportion of total reservation transactions.

CHANNELS OR SOURCES OF RESERVATION

The following are the channels and sources of reservation of hotel guestrooms: -

1. Hotels / Motels :

- The hotels and motels are the main sources or channels of reservation for guests as the guests can directly approach the guests for the process of reservation of guestrooms.

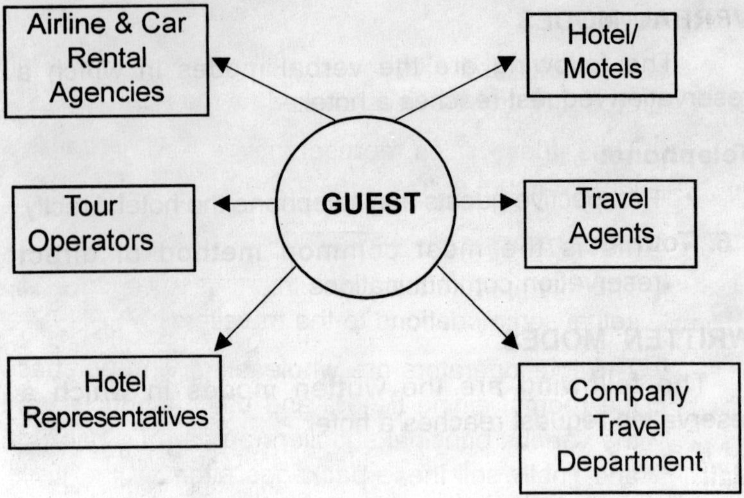

- Thus, the guests can personally visit the hotels and motels for reservation or may even contact these properties through telephone, fax, e-mail etc.

2. Travel Agents :

- The travel agents are also and important channels or sources of reservation for the hospitality properties.
- The travel agents are intermediary retail agents who sell rooms, airline seats and other products and services to the travellers.

3. Company Travel Departments :

- Most of the big corporate organizations have a separate travel departments consisting of hired professionals who arrange and cater for the travel and accommodation requirements of the travellers.

4. Hotel Representatives :

- All the hospitality properties have sales representatives who approach various market segments and give the sales presentations of the products and services offered by the hotels.

- Thus, these sales representatives also generate a large amount of revenue for the hotel.

5. Tour Operators :

- The tour operators are also intermediary agents who sell accommodations to the travellers.
- The tour operators are wholesalers who purchase the rooms, airline tickets and other products from the various principal suppliers and form a package and finally sell these packages either to the travel agents or to the guest directly.
- Thus, the price quoted by the wholesalers is always less than the price quoted by the travel agents.

6. Airline And Car Rental Agencies :

- The airline agencies are also principal suppliers who act as intermediary agents for the hotels and help these hospitality properties to sell their products such as rooms along with the airline seats which they sell to the travellers.

TYPES OF RESERVATION

Reservation

It is a mutual agreement between the guest and the hotel in which the guest hires accommodation from the hotel at a given time for a given time.

Guaranteed Reservation

- A guaranteed reservation assures the guest that the hotel will hold a room until a specific time (check-out time) of the day following the guest's scheduled arrival date.

Types of Reservation

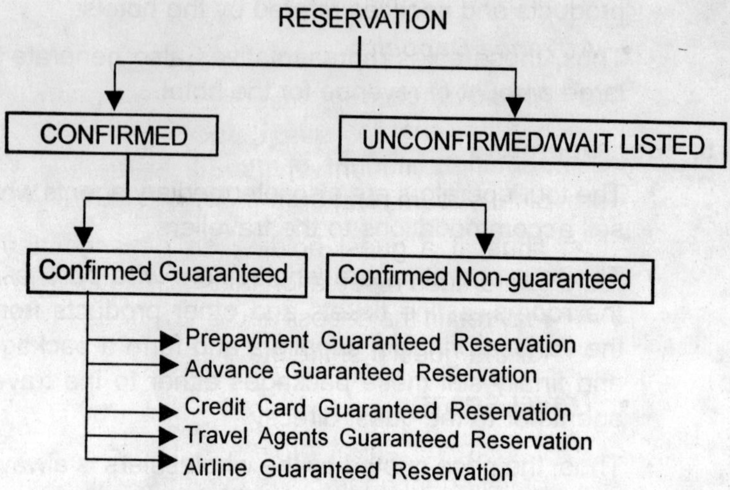

- The guest in turn, guarantees to pay for the room, even it is not used.
- Thus, the guaranteed reservations provide some protection for the hotel's revenue even in the case of no-show, a situation in which a guest makes a reservation but does not register or cancel.

Types of Guaranteed Reservation

- ***Prepayment:***
  - A prepayment guaranteed reservation requires that a payment in full be received before the day of the arrival of the guest.
  - This type of reservation is the most desirable form of reservation and is used at the resorts.
- ***Credit Card:***
  - A credit card guaranteed reservation is a type of guaranteed reservation in which a credit card

company ensures that the lodging properties will receive payment for the no-shows.

- ***Advance Deposit:***
  - An advance deposit guaranteed reservation requires that the guest should pay the hotel a specified amount of money as deposit (one night's room rent) before arrival.
  - Thus, if a guest holding an advance deposit guaranteed reservation fails to register, the hotel may retain the deposit and cancel the reservation for the guest's entire stay.
- ***Travel Agent:***
  - In a travel agent guaranteed reservation, the travel agent guarantees the guest's reservation.
  - Thus, in case of a no-show, the hotel generally bills the travel agency for the payment and the travel agent must then collect from the client or the guest.
- ***Voucher or Miscellaneous Charge Order:***
  - The voucher or the miscellaneous charge order is issued by the Airline Reporting Corporation (ARC).
  - Thus, in this case the ARC guarantees payment to the hotel if the travel agency defaults on payment or if the guest is a no-show.
- ***Corporate:***
  - A corporate guaranteed reservation involves a corporation or a company entering in to a contract with the hotel and will accept the financial responsibility for any no-show business travellers the company sponsors.

Non-guaranteed Reservation

- A non-guaranteed reservation assures the guest that the hotel will hold a room until a stated reservation cancellation hour on the day of arrival.
- This type of reservation does not guarantee that the property will receive payment for no-shows.
- Thus, if the guest does not arrive by the cancellation hour, the hotel is free to release the room for sale.
- If the guest arrives after the cancellation hour, the hotel will accommodate the guest if a room is available.

SYSTEMS OF RESERVATION

The following are the various systems of reservation in the hotel industry: -

1. Hotel Diary System of Reservation

- The hotel diary system of reservation is found in hotels which are small in size and thus, have limited number of guestrooms with them (15-20 rooms).
- This system consists of a booking diary which is maintained by the reservation office and is used for taking down the reservations for the coming or future period.
- The booking diary has got 365 to 366 pages which mark the days of the year.
- Each page is for each day of the year for which guestrooms of the hotel will be reserved.
- Thus, the reservations are taken for the requested date in reservation and then transferred to the diary according to the date of arrival of the guest.
- The diary also contains various other information which are taken from the guest at the time

reservation such as duration of stay, room type and plan requested, name of the guest, PAX, mode of payment and special instructions.

Advantages:

i. It is useful for small hotels.

ii. All the information is available at one place together and so the chance for losing information is very less.

Disadvantages:

i. As the diary is big and heavy, its movement is difficult.

ii. Cancellations and amendments can create problem and disturb the sequence of the diary.

2. Whitney System of Reservation

- The Whitney system of reservation was a very popular system of processing reservation in large hotels which had non-automated operating system.
- The Whitney system of reservation consists of a large wooden rack called the "*Whitney Rack*" which has 14 to 16 columns.
- Each of these columns has a number of metallic pockets for storing the reservation information in Whitney slips.
- The first column is the broadest and stores the reservation of the present month of the present year.
- The next 11 columns denote the forthcoming eleven columns of the present and the next year.
- The last 2 columns are for the subsequent years to come.
- Thus, the reservation information is transferred to the Whitney slips from the reservation form and then, the Whitney slips are arranged according date of arrival in the columns.

Advantages:

i. It is useful for taking reservations in large hotels.

ii. Cancellations and amendments are very easy as the slips can be easily referred.

Disadvantages:

i. The Whitney slips may be lost and the reservation information can be lost.

3. Central Reservation System

- The central reservation system is a fully computerized network of reservation used by the players of the hospitality industry across the world.
- The central reservation system operates through the satellite and is based on the principle of WAN (Wide Area Network).
- The central reservation system operates through Central Reservation Offices which are also called CROs.
- The following are the main types of Central Reservation System: -

I. *Affiliate Central Reservation System :*

- The affiliate central reservation system is the central reservation network formed by the properties of a particular hotel chain.
- The reservation system operates through the central reservation offices which are located within the properties of the chain, outside the hotel in the same city and also in cities where the particular chain is not having any such property.
- Thus, through the central reservation system, a guest can book his reservation from one city to another as well as from cities where the chain has no properties.

- Thus, it is important for the participating properties of the chain to give their room availability to the central reservation offices from time to time.
- Sometimes, independent properties also participate in the affiliate reservation system of a particular chain in order to gain the benefit of the central reservation network and so these independent properties are called **Overflow Facility**.

II. ***Non-affiliate Central Reservation System:*** -

- The non-affiliate central reservation system is formed by the association of the independent properties in order to gain the same benefits of the affiliate central reservation system.
- The non-affiliate central reservation system also works in the same way as the affiliate central reservation system.

4. Instant Reservation System

- The Instant Reservation System is also a fully computerized reservation network and is also based on the principle of Wide Area Network.
- The Instant Reservation System operates through the Instant Reservation Offices which are also called IROs.
- The Instant Reservation Offices are always located in the hotels of the chain forming the IRS.
- The IRO is a separate office other than the hotel's own reservation office and the IRO takes or accepts the reservation request of all the other participating properties of the reservation network except the property in which it is located as the reservation office of the particular property takes its reservation requests.

- The IRS, thus, has got a limited coverage and thus are used by hotel chains which cannot afford to establish a central reservation system due to heavy installation expenditure.

CANCELLATIONS, AMENDMENTS AND OVERBOOKING

Reservation Maintenance

- Most of the time it becomes necessary for the hotel to make modifications to the reservations of the guests or to cancel the reservation as requested by the guest.
- Thus, it is very important for the reservation department to properly maintain the various reservations of the guests for future amendments or cancellation.
- Thus, a reservation agent should be efficient enough to organize and properly keep a track of the reservation records of the guests.
- Thus, if a person contacts the hotel to change a reservation, the reservations agent must be able to quickly trace the reservation record of the guest, verify its details and do the needful modification.

Modifying Non-guaranteed Reservations

- Guests often make non-guaranteed reservation for their stay as they are mostly sure that they will reach the property before the stated cancellation hour of the hotel.
- Sometimes, it happens that the guests are not able to arrive on time at the hotel. In that case, most of the guests convert their non-guaranteed reservation into a guaranteed one.

- The following is the procedure to modify a non-guaranteed reservation: -
    - Obtain the name of the guest and find out the correct non-guaranteed reservation record.
    - Obtain the guest's credit card type, number and expiration date and the cardholder's name, and verify the validity of the credit card.
    - Assign the guest, a new reservation confirmation number according to the policy of the hotel.
    - Complete the change from non-guaranteed to guaranteed reservation status according to the procedures of the property.

Reservation Cancellation

- A reservation cancellation by the guests informs the reservation department that a particular room is again available on a particular date for the guest.
- It is extremely important for the hotels to properly process the reservation cancellation and the reservation agent should be very courteous to the guests while handling the reservation cancellation.

Cancelling a Non-guaranteed Reservation

- To cancel a non-guaranteed reservation, the reservations agent should obtain the name and address of the guest, number of rooms reserved by the guest, scheduled date of arrival and departure.
- This information will make sure that the correct reservation record is found out and cancelled.
- After recording the cancellation, the reservations agent should assign a cancellation number to the guest.

Cancelling a Credit Card Guaranteed Reservation

- To cancel a credit card guaranteed reservation, obtain the total information about the guest reservation related to the guest stay such as date of arrival and departure, name and address of the guest and reservation number.
- Mark the reservation as cancelled and add the cancellation number to the reservation record. If someone other than the guest makes the cancellation, the reservations agent should add the caller's name to the cancelled reservation record.

Cancelling an Advance Deposit Guaranteed Reservation

- Cancelling an advanced deposit guaranteed reservation vary according to the policy of the hotel.
- The reservations agent should take extreme care while cancelling the advance deposit guaranteed reservation as this cancellation deals with cash deposit.
- Deposits are normally returned to guests who properly cancel the reservation.

Cancelling other Guaranteed Reservation

- Generally it is the representative of the company or the travel agency who contacts the hotel to cancel a corporate account or travel agency guaranteed reservation.
- It is important to enter the name of the person cancelling the reservation on the reservation record.
- A reservation cancellation number should be issued in both the cases and should be recorded.

Overbooking

- Overbooking is a process of accepting more number of reservations than the actual number of guestrooms present in the hotel.
- This is not an error but is rather an action taken by the front office management in order to reduce losses to the hotel due to no-shows and cancellations.
- No-shows are guests who do not register in a hotel even after having a confirmed reservation and neither do they cancel their reservation. So, these guests cause a loss to the hotel and reduce the revenue for the hotel. Thus, overbooking is done in order to reduce the impact of the no-shows on the revenue of the hotel.
- Cancellations are guests who cancel their reservations either well before time or even at the last time and thus, the last minute cancellations also cause a lot of problem to the hotel management and reduce the overall revenue of the hotel. Thus, overbooking is done in order to reduce the impact of the cancellations on the revenue of the hotel.
- Thus, overbooking is a very complicated process and should be done in a cautious manner on the base of the history of reservation trends as improper overbooking can lead the hotel to a situation where the hotel has no choice but to bounce guests due to full house condition.

6

REGISTRATION

THE SIX STEPS OF REGISTRATION PROCESS

Definition and Purpose of Registration

- The process of assigning a guestroom to a guest and checking him in after the completion of other legal formalities (*establishing the method of payment and creating a registration record*) on his arrival is called registration.
- Registration serves three main purposes:
  - It satisfies the legal requirements.
  - It provides a record of actual arrival as opposed to bookings. The traditional justification for registration was that it provided some form of record in the case of a fire or any other natural disaster.
  - It helps to confirm the guest's acceptance of the hotel's terms and conditions, and is thus useful should legal proceedings be necessary.

The Steps of the Registration Process

- The following are the six main steps of the registration process of a guest:

- Preregistration activity
- Creation of the registration record
- Assignment of the room and rate
- Establishment of the method of payment
- Issual of the room key
- Fulfillment of special requests

PRE-REGISTRATION ACTIVITY

Description of the Pre-registration Process

- Preregistration activities are the registration activities that occur before the guests arrive at the property (generally one day in advance) and are primarily aimed at saving their time during the registration process.
- Thus, the guest can be pre-registered using the information collected by reservations agents during the reservations process and so the pre-registered only need to verify information already entered on to a registration card and pro vide a valid signature in the appropriate place on the registration card.
- Preregistration generally involves production of a registration card, room and rate assignment, creation of a guest folio and some other function in advance of the guest arrival.
- In non-automated and semi-automated systems, the pre-registration activities are carried manually while in the fully automated systems; the pre-registration activities are carried in computers.

Advantages of the Pre-registration Process

- Preregistration helps to plan for special requirements of guests as well as of the hotel such as requirement of special rooms for the disabled and sick guests.

- Preregistration helps managers to know about the day when the hotel will be at full occupancy over the next several days.
- Preregistration helps the guests to experience innovative registration options, e.g. Registration in the van sent for airport pickup.

CREATION OF THE REGISTRATION RECORD

- After the arrival of the guest in a hotel, the front office agent creates a registration record, which is a collection of important guest information.
- The registration cards facilitate the registration process in non-automated and semi-automated hotels.
- The registration card requires the guest to provide his or her name, address, telephone number, company affiliation and other personal data.
- The registration card usually contains a space for the guest's signature, which is a legal requirement in most of the hotels to establish a guest relationship with the hotel.
- Even in automated properties, guests are generally asked to sign a pre-printed registration card to verify the accuracy of the registration document.
- The registration cards, or their computer-generated equivalent, require the guests to indicate their intended method of settlement for rooms and other hotel goods and services and also require the guests to confirm their assigned room rate and their departure date.
- Many registration cards contain an acknowledgement on the part of the guest that he or she will abide by the rules of the hotel regarding payment and other aspects for a comfortable stay.

- The guests arriving in the hotel without a reservation (***walk-ins***) have to undergo a different registration procedure. The front office agent collects the entire guest data during the registration itself and feed those data in the computer terminal.
- At checkout, the information captured on a guest's registration card may be used as the primary source for creating a guest history record which then becomes a part of the data base to be used in the future by the hotel's sales and marketing efforts.

ASSIGNMENT OF ROOM AND RATE

- Room assignment is an important part of the registration process and involves identifying and allocating an available room in a specific room rate category to a guest.
- On the basis of reservation information, specific rooms may be assigned before the arrival of the guest depending on the rooms forecasted availability status and how appropriately the room meets the guest's needs.
- When the guests arrive they would require the rooms as quickly as possible. If they arrive before mid-day, then it is unlikely that the rooms will be ready unless they are vacant from the previous night.
- In smaller hotels, the allocation of rooms is normally done at the time of booking, by using the conventional chart. If when a guest arrives the room allocated is not ready, but a similar one is, then the chart has to be changed round to show the re-allocation.
- VIPs and guests with special requirements are pre-allocated the rooms in order to save their valuable time.
- In allocating rooms the receptionist should aim to satisfy tne guests as much as possible. Allocation

should take place on the basis of putting the guests who are staying the longest into the best rooms and guests who booked first in to rooms better than those who booked at the last moment.

- A hotel that operates a computerized system will ensure that the package carries provision for different tariffs, locations and individual guest preferences. The computer will select the best available room for a particular reservation, or offer alternatives if the preferred is already taken or not yet ready. It is extremely essential that the package is flexible enough to ensure that any special requests by guests can be catered for.

The assignment of the room rate:

- A room rate is the price the hotel charges for overnight accommodations. The cost structure of the hotel sets the floor to the price for a room, and competition sets the ceiling to the price by establishing the maximum room rate.
- A hotel will usually designate a standard rate for each room. This rate is typically called the rack rate because traditionally the standard rate was the one posted on or near the room rack. The rack is considered the retail rate for the room. So, the discounts provided by the hotels are mostly on the rack rate.
- Room rates are generally assigned during the reservation process except for ***walk-ins*** who are assigned the room rates only during the registration process.
- Front desk agents are often allowed to offer discounts to the guests during reservation or registration and thus they can offer a room at a lower price than its standard rack rate when the

management thinks it is appropriate.

- Hotels also offer seasonal rates to provide greater value to the guests during the low demand periods and to maximise the room revenue during the high demand periods. (***a type of revenue management***)
- Room rates may also vary based on the type of guests. The front office agent should know how and when to apply a special room rate during registration.

ESTABLISHMENT OF THE METHOD OF PAYMENT

- The establishment of the method of settlement of the bill by the guest during the stay is an important part of the registration process.
- The creation of the guest folio is an essential step of the registration process of the guest in a hotel.
- Regardless of whether the guest intends to pay by cash, check, credit card, or any other acceptable method, the hotel should take precautionary measures to ensure payment.
- Effective account settlement depends on the steps taken during registration to determine the guest's method of payment.
- Thus, the registration process plays an important part in front guest accounting since the front desk agents are responsible for collecting information on the intended method of payment during check-in.

Cash:

- Many guests prefer to pay the guestroom charges during registration, in advance of their stay in the hotel.

- Thus, the guests who pay cash for their stay in advance are not extended or given any credit facilities.
- The revenue centres are well notified of the list of PIA guests in order to avoid posting any charges to their account. (***no post status***)
- So, these guests have to settle their bill at the point of purchase the moment they purchase any service.

Personal Cheques:

- Most of the hotels do not consider personal cheques as a very acceptable method of payment.
- Although a hotel has no legal obligation to accept cheques, they cannot refuse the payment through cheques on the basis of illegal reasons.
- Hotels must consider policies relative to payroll cheques, personal cheques written on out-of-state and foreign bank accounts, government checks, and second-and third-party cheques.
- Nowadays most of the hotels require cheque guarantee cards for accepting the personal cheques.

Second- and Third- Party Cheques:

- In general, hotels do not accept a second- or a third-party cheque.
- A second-party cheque is one made out to the guest presenting the cheque.
- A third-party cheque is a cheque made out to someone who has in turn signed the cheque over to the guest presenting it.

- The hotels generally do not accept these cheques in order to avoid any type of collection problems.

Credit Card:

- Charge cards are different in number of ways.
- The customer has to pay an annual subscription for the cards and has to settle each month's settlement in full.
- There are no facilities for extending repayment. Generally, the credit limit on charge cards will be higher, and they are likely to be used for the purchase of airline tickets, hotel bills and restaurant bills, and also as company charge cards.
- All major card companies operate a 24-hour authorisation centre where a cashier may make a reverse charge call to check on the validity of the card or obtain clearance to accept payment of bill above the "floor limit'.
- Many front office departments of hotels keep "stop list' of lost or stolen cards.

PROCEDURE OF PAYMENT BY CREDIT CARD:

- Check that the bill is inside the "floor limit".
- Obtain the card from the client.
- Swipe the card through the machine.
- Ask the client to sign the audit roll (retain the card).
- Check that the signatures on the card and the voucher agree.
- Return the card and the top copy to the guest.

In the case of a hotel operating a system that does have EPOS, it will be necessary to prepare a sales voucher manually, and take an imprint of the client's card on the machine provided.

ISSUAL OF THE ROOM KEY

- The front office agent completes the registration process by issuing the room key to the guest.
- Some hotels enclose the room key in a key card for the purpose of security. These key cards have the room numbers written or printed on them.
- Some hotels even hand over a copy of the hotel map and brochure for the sake of convenience of the guest.
- The guest is finally escorted with his luggage to his room by a bell-person, who also explains the special features of the hotel to the guest.

Key Control:

- One of reception's important jobs have been issuing room keys to the guests and them take them back for safe keeping when the guests went out.
- The keys had a large and heavy tags attached to them to stop gusts from walking off with them.
- The tags were numbered so that the keys could be hung on a ***"key rack"*** when not in use. The key rack was usually situated behind the desk.
- The old fashioned metal key was a security risk. Guests often missed or mislaid them.
- Thus the modern hotels started using electronic keys as a solution to the problem. These keys were made of plastic and punched or magnetically coded with the door code.
- These keys do not have the room number printed on them, so the guest has to be given an additional key card showing this.

- So, the guest has to keep this card separate from the electronic room key in case the latter is stolen.
- The room lock is programmed to accept only the code on the electronic key, which is changed every time the room is let.

Electronic Key Card System:

- An electronic locking system replaces traditional mechanical locks with sophisticated computer-based guestroom access devices.
- A centralized locking system operates through a master control console at the front desk which is wired to every guestroom door.
- At registration, a front desk agent inserts a key or card in to the appropriate room slot at the front desk console to transmit its code to the guestroom door lock.
- These locks can be designed to use a magnetic key card or a special high-security card.

Advantages of the Electronic Keys:

- These electronic keys are relatively cheaper than the metal keys, so their loss does not matter much.
- These electronic keys have cut down the number of thefts from rooms by a significant amount.
- They have eliminated the time wasting process of taking keys in and handling them out.
- Thus they allow the receptionist to concentrate on productive contacts with guests.

FULFILLMENT OF SPECIAL REQUESTS

- It is extremely important for the front office agents to pay attention to the special requests made by the guests during registration for acknowledgement.

- The front desk agent should mention the guest's special requests at check-in to make sure that the hotel has provided what the guest requested.
- If it appears that the special requests made by the guests during reservation have not been made, the front desk agent should try his or her best to meet these requests during the registration of the guests.
- The following are the some examples of special requests made by the guests:

Location : The guests may request for rooms close to the elevator or the Emergency exit or far from the elevators.

View : The guests may request for rooms either facing the swimming

Bed type : The guests may request for rooms with extra bed or a crib for children.

Amenities : The guests may even request for special amenities such as iron And ironing boards, additional pillows, additional cloth hangers, audiovisual and office equipment.

Special furnishings : Disabled guests may require rooms

For disabled guests : with certain design features such as grab bars in the bath tub or special lights attached to smoke and fire detection systems.

WHEN THE GUESTS CANNOT BE ACCOMMODATED

Walk-in Guests

- The hotels have no obligations towards the walk-in guests who come to hotel without reservation and demand room.
- Hotels have no obligations to accommodate the walk-in guests when rooms are available in the hotel due to full occupancy.
- If a walk-in guest cannot be accommodated, the front desk agents can make the situation a little easier for the guest by suggesting and providing directions to alternative hotels nearby.
- The front office agent may even offer to call another hotel to assist the guest.
- Hotels should keep a list, with phone numbers, of comparable properties in the area.

When the Walk-in Guests Claim that They have Guaranteed Reservation

- If the guests presents a letter of confirmation, verify the date and the name of the hotel; the guest may have arrived on a different date or at the wrong property. Most confirmation letters have a confirmation number, which will help the front desk agent locate the reservation record.
- Ask whether another person might have made the reservation for the guest; the reservation may be at another property, or it may be misfiled under the caller's name, not the guest's name.
- Re-check the reservation file or computer system in view of the guest; perhaps the reservation was incorrectly filed or otherwise mishandled.

- Double-check the reservation file for another spelling of the guest's last name. Also, check to see if the guest's first and last names were inadvertently reversed in the reservation file.
- If the reservation was made through a travel agency or representative, allow the guest to call the originating source for clarification.
- Ask the guest to confirm his or her arrival date; the guest may be arriving on a different day or a day date. Many hotels hold no-show registration cards from the previous day in the front of the registration file just in case a no-show arrives a day date.
- If there seems to be alternative to walking (turning away) the guest, a manager, not a front desk agent, should explain the matter in a private office. Registering one guest in view of another who cannot be accommodated can be extremely awkward and embarrassing.

Guests with Non-guaranteed Reservations

- A number of situations or circumstances can delay a guest's scheduled arrival.
- Guests frequently do not have the chance to change a non-guaranteed reservation to a guaranteed reservation by the time they realize they will arrive past the hotel's reservation cancellation hour.
- As a result, the hotel may not hold the room for the guest and may have a room available when the guest arrives.
- If a hotel cannot provide a guestroom, front office management extremely careful when informing the guest.
- The blame should be placed on either side since the lack of accommodations is neither the fault of the hotel nor the fault of the guest.

GUESTS WITH GUARANTEED RESERVATIONS

- Review all front desk transactions to ensure full occupancy.
- Re-take an accurate count of rooms occupied, using all relevant data.
- Compare the room rack, housekeeper's report, and guest folios for any discrepancy in occupancy status.
- Telephone due-outs who have not yet checked out and confirm their departure time.
- Personally check the current status of rooms listed as out-of-order. Perhaps an out-of-order room might be readied for sale. If a guest is willing to occupy an out-of –order room its rate could be adjusted.
- Identify the rooms pre-blocked for one or two days in the future and pre register the guest arriving the present day who depart in time to honour the block.

7

FRONT OFFICE COORDINATION

INTERDEPARTMENTAL COORDINATION OF FRONT OFFICE

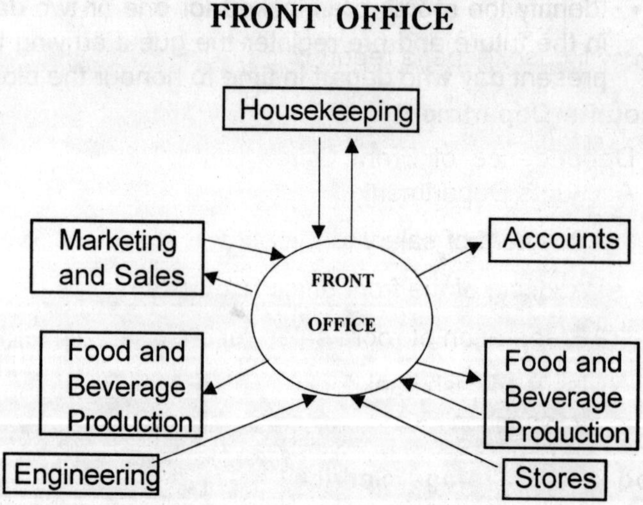

The following are the main departments with which the front office coordinates during the operation in hotels: -

1. Housekeeping Department

a) Dependence of Housekeeping on the Front Office Department

- Groups and VIPs rooming list
- Arrival notification
- Departure notification
- Room change notification
- Room discrepancy front office report (*in case of skipper*)

b) Dependence of Front Office Department on the Housekeeping Department

- Clean and vacant guestrooms
- Intimation of Out Of Order guestrooms
- Housekeeper's report of the guestroom status

2. Accounts Department

a) Dependence of Front Office Department on the Accounts Department

- Payment of salary to the staff
- Auditing of the front office accounts
- Preparation of room sales report
- Issue of cash bank for carrying out the front office transaction

3. Food and Beverage Service

a) Dependence of Food and Beverage Service Department on the Front Office Department

- Groups and VIPs rooming list
- Arrival notification
- Departure notification

- Room change notification
- Issue of amenities voucher

b) Dependence of Front Office Department on the Food and Beverage Service Department

- Provision of food and beverage service to the guests in the guestrooms as well as in other food and beverage outlets of the hotel.

4. Stores

a) Dependence of Front Office Department on the Stores

- Issue of stationery for the staff
- Issue of formats and reports for carrying out the operations of the front office

5. Engineering and Maintenance Department

a) Dependence of Front Office Department on the Engineering and Maintenance Department

- Maintenance of Out Of Order guestrooms
- Manufacturing of duplicate guestroom keys
- Maintenance of the front office keys equipments such as bell trolley

6. Food and Beverage Production Department

a) Dependence of Food and Beverage Production Department on the Front Office Department

- Groups and VIPs rooming list
- Arrival notification
- Departure notification
- Room change notification
- Issue of amenities voucher

7. Marketing and Sales Department

a) Dependence of Marketing and Sales Department on the Front Office Department

- Room forecast information to the marketing and sales department

b) Dependence of Front Office Department on the Marketing and Sales Department

- Suggestions to improve the room sales strategies of the front office department
- Information about new agreements made with companies and airlines regarding accommodation

8

ON-GOING RESPONSIBILITIES

COMMUNICATION WITH FRONT OFFICE

Log Book

- The front office generally maintains a log book, which is an important format which makes the front office staff aware of important events and decisions that occurred during previous workshifts.
- A typical front office log book is a daily journal, which chronicles unusual events, guest complaints or requests, and other relevant information.
- The front desk agents record in the log book throughout their shift. These notes should be clearly written in a prescribed form so that they serve as effective reference material for the next shift.
- Before the beginning of the shift, front desk supervisors and agents should review and initial log book, noting any current activities, situations that require follow-up or potential problems.
- The front office is important for the management as it helps the management to understand the activity of the front desk and it records any ongoing issues.

Information Directory

- The front office staff must be able to respond in a knowledgeable way when guests contact the front desk for information.
- Some front offices accumulate such data in a bound guide called an information directory.
- The following are the main information provided by the information directory: -
  - Local restaurant recommendations.
  - Contacting a taxi company.
  - Directions to the local companies.
  - Directions to the nearest shopping center, drug store, etc.
  - Directions to the nearest places of worship.
  - Directions to the nearest bank or the automated teller machine.
  - Direction to the theater, stadium, or ticket agency.
  - Directions to the universities, libraries, museums, or other points of local interest.
  - Directions to the local courts or the city hall.
  - Information about the hotel policies.
  - Information about the hotel's recreational facilities or those near the hotel.
- Some hotels have installed computer information terminals in public areas including the lobby area.
- These terminals are essentially an electronic equivalent of the front office information directory.
- Guests without front office assistance easily access computer-based information terminals.

- In addition, many hotels provide a printed schedule of daily events or display a daily event board through a closed-circuit television system.
- A common industry term for displaying daily events is the reader board. Printed itineraries may be place at the front desk, in elevators, and throughout the lobby area.

Mail and Packaging Handling

- Registered guests rely on the front office to relay delivered mail and packages quickly and efficiently.
- Front office managers normally develop policies for mail and package handling based on the policies and regulations of the Indian Postal Department.
- In general, the front office is expected to time-stamp all guest mail when it arrives at the property. This answers any question arising regarding when the mail arrive at the property or how quickly the guest was noticed about its arrival.
- When the mail and packages arrives, the front office record should be checked to verify that the guest is about to arrive, is currently registered in the hotel or has departed from the hotel.

Handling of Normal Mails

- Mail for Registered Guests: -
  1. Usually, mail for a registered guest is held in the appropriate room slot in a mail and message rack or in an alphabetical rack by the guest's last name.
  2. The front office should promptly notify the guest that a mail has been received from his behalf. Some properties notify the guests by switching on an in-room message light on the guestroom

telephone; others deliver a printed form to the telephone.

- Mail for guests who have not yet arrived: -
  1. If a mail arrives for a guest who has not yet registered, a notation should be made on the guest's reservation record.
  2. The mail safely kept in a drawer until the guest arrives.
- Mail for guests whop has already checked-out: -
  1. Guest mail that is not picked up or has arrived for a guest who has already checked out should be time stamped a second time and returned to its sender or sent to a forwarding address if the guest has provided one.

Handling of Registered Mail

- Guests may also receive registered letters, express mail packages, or other mail requiring a signature on delivery.
- Some hotels permit the front desk agent to sign for such mail.
- Then, the agent records the item's delivery in the front office mail signature book, and has the guest sign for the mail in the book at the time of pick-up or delivery.

Handling of Packages

- Packages are usually handled as mail. If the package is too large to store at the front desk, it should be taken to a secure room.
- The package and its location should be recorded in the front office mail signature book.
- When mail or packages are received, it is customary to notify the guest immediately.

GUEST SERVICES

- As the center of front office activity, the front desk is responsible for co-coordinating the guest services.
- Typical guest services involve providing information and special equipments and supplies.
- Guest services may also include accommodating guests through special procedures.
- A request that is beyond the responsibility of the front office should be directly referred to the appropriate department.
- A growing number of hotels employ a concierge or other designated staff member to handle guest requests.

Equipment and Supplies

- Guests may request special equipment and supplies while making a reservation , at the time of registration, or during occupancy.
- Reservation agents should have a reliable method of recording the special requests to ensure that they are properly met.
- After registration, a guest who needs special equipment or supplies will almost always contact a front desk agent.
- Equipment and supplies commonly requested by the guests include: -

  a) Roll-away beds and cribs

  b) Additional linens / pillows

  c) Irons and ironing boards

  d) Additional cloth hangers

e) Audiovisual and office equipment

f) Special equipment for visually impaired, or physically challenged guests.

- The front desk agents should have alternative ways to meet guest requests when the department that normally provides the equipment or services is closed or inaccessible.
- In many hotels the front desk agent have the accessibility to the linen and housekeeping supplies room to provide the guests with the equipments required by them in the absence of any housekeeping staff.

Special Procedures

- The guests may ask for special treatment when making a reservation, during registration, at the time of check-out or during occupancy.
- The reservation agents should have a reliable method of recording special requests made during the process of reservation and communicating such requests to appropriate front office staff.
- The front office staff should be empowered to handle the request and satisfy the guest if at all possible.
- Procedural requests may require more time and effort to fulfill than equipment and supply requests. Typical procedural request include: -

a) Split account folios:

This is generally requested by the business travellers to separate the room charges and taxes from the other charges such as food and beverage charges because some companies pay only the accommodation charges of their employees.

b) Master account folios:

This is generally requested by a convention group meeting to post only the authorized charges incurred in the hotel in to the master folio.

c) Wake-up calls:

The wake-up calls are requested by the guest requiring to perform some important tasks such as catching a flight early in the morning.

d) Transportation arrangements:

The guests may also require various transportation services from the hotel during arrival, occupancy or during their departure.

e) Newspaper delivery and secretarial services:

- A concierge may handle other procedural requests. Hotels not employing a concierge have a front desk agent to handle these requests.
- Some hotels operate a guest service center to handle the various special and procedural requests of the guests.

GUEST RELATIONS AND COMPLAINT HANDLING

Guest Relation

- The front office should develop strategies and tactics in anticipation of complaints made by the guest to resolve the situation and satisfy the guest.
- The high visibility of the front office means that front desk agents are the first to learn about the guest complaints.
- The front desk agent should always attentively listen to complaints made by the guest and seek a timely resolution to the problem.

- Employees should also realize that the guests who do not have the opportunity to complain often tell their friends, relatives and business associate about this.
- When the guests find it easy to express their opinions, both the hotel and the guest benefit. The hotel learns of potential or actual problems and has the opportunity to resolve them thus satisfying the guest.
- When the problems are easily resolved, the guest thinks that the hotel cares about his needs.

Complaints Handling

- There are four categories of problems associated complaints: -

a) Mechanical Complaints:

- Most guest complaints relate to the malfunction of the hotel equipments.
- This generally include problems with climate control, lighting, electricity, room furnishings, ice machines, vending machines, door keys, plumbing, television sets, elevators and so on.
- Effective use of the log book and maintenance work orders may reduce the frequency of the mechanical complaints.
- It is therefore required that appropriate staff member should be should be dispatched as quickly as possible with the proper tools to fix the problem.

b) Attitudinal Complaints:

- The guests may make attitudinal complaints when they feel insulted by rude behavior of the staffs.
- Guests who overhear staff conversations or who complaints from the hotel staff members may also express attitudinal complaints.

- Managers and supervisors should listen and attend to the complaints and problems of staff. This can be especially critical to maintain solid guest relations.

c) ***Service-related Complaints:***

- Guests make service-related complaints when they experience a problem with hotel service.
- Service –related complaints may be wide-ranging and may include long waiting time for service, lack of assistance with luggage, untidy rooms, phone difficulties, missed wake-up calls, cold or ill-prepared food, or ignored request for additional supplies.

d) ***Unusual Complaints:***

- Guests may also complaint about the absence of swimming pool, lack of transportation services and bad weather and so on.
- Hotels have little or no control over the situations involving unusual complaints.
- The front office management should therefore alert front desk agents that on occasion guest may complain about the things a staff can do nothing.
- Through such orientation, staff will be better prepared to handle an unusual situation with appropriate guest relations techniques and avoid a potentially difficult encounter.

- **The following are the guidelines, a front office management and staff should keep while handling the guest complaints: -**
    - When expressing a complaint, the guest may be quite angry. Front office staff members should

not go alone to a guestroom to investigate a problem or otherwise risk potential danger.

- Front office staff members should not make promises that exceed their authority.
- If a problem cannot be solved, front office staff should admit this to the guest early on. Honesty is the best policy when dealing with guest complaints.
- Front desk agents should be advised that some guests complain as part of their nature, the front office should develop an approach for dealing with such guests.

Follow-up Procedures

- Front office management may use the front office log book to initiate corrective action, verify that the guest complaints have been resolved, and identify recurring problems.
- This written record may also enable management to contact guests who may still be dissatisfied with some aspect of their stay at check-out.
- After the guest has departed, a letter from the front office manager expressing regret about the about the incident can promote the goodwill of the hotel.
- It may be step from the part of the front office manager to telephone a departed guest to get a more complete description of the incident.
- Chain hotels may also receive guest complaints channeled through chain headquarters.
- Records of guest complaints about eh hotels in the chain may be compiled and sent to each manager.
- This method of feedback allows the chin's corporate headquarters to evaluate and compare each hotel's guest relations performance.

Handling Complaints

Housekeeping

- The housekeeping department and the front office must keep each other informed of changes in room status to ensure that guests are roomed efficiently and without complication.
- The more familiar front office staffs are with housekeeping procedures, and vice versa, the sooner the relationship will be between the two departments.

Enginerring And Maintenance

- In many hotels, engineering and maintenance personnel begin each shift by examining the front office log book for repair work orders.
- Front desk agents use the log book to track maintenance problems reported by guests or staff, such as poor heating or cooling, faulty plumbing, noisy equipment, or broken furniture.
- The front office log book serves as an excellent reference for hotel's engineering and maintenance staff.
- If a maintenance problem renders a room unsalable, housekeeping must be informed immediately when the problem is resolved so the room can be placed back in the available room inventory.

9

DURING THE STAY ACTIVITIES

INFORMATION SERVICES

The Information Desk

- The Information Desk of the front office is also an important section of the department and plays an important role in give the guests and visitors valuable information about the hotel and the city at large.
- The information desk is operated by a Concierge who is also known as the information assistant.
- The concierge provides important information to the guests and the visitors about the various facilities and services of the hotel and also gives important information about the city such as the routes to the nearest airport or railway station or hospitals and banks.
- The concierge also plays an important in arranging tickets for the guests in various concerts taking place in the city.

Information Directory

- The front office staff must be able to respond in a

knowledgeable way when guests contact the front desk for information.

- Some front offices accumulate such data in a bound guide called an information directory.
- The following are the main information provided by the information directory: -
    - Local restaurant recommendations.
    - Contacting a taxi company.
    - Directions to the local companies.
    - Directions to the nearest shopping center, drug store, etc.
    - Directions to the nearest places of worship.
    - Directions to the nearest bank or the automated teller machine.
    - Direction to the theater, stadium, or ticket agency.
    - Directions to the universities, libraries, museums, or other points of local interest.
    - Directions to the local courts or the city hall.
    - Information about the hotel policies.
    - Information about the hotel's recreational facilities or those near the hotel.

Readers Board

- The Reader's Board is a very important tool of providing information to the guests, visitors and patrons of the hotel.
- The Reader's Board is located in the lobby of the hotel and consists of a velvet board with a golden metallic boarder and the board is fixed with the help of a stand.

- The board shows all the current events which are presently taking place in the hotel such as wedding ceremonies in the banquets, meetings, conferences and other important official events, festivals and exhibitions taking place in the hotel.
- The events are shown on the board with golden alphabets on a red velvet background and thus, are clearly visible to the guests, patrons and visitors to the hotel.

Tent Card

- The tent card is also a very important tool of promoting the hotel to the in-house guests of the hotel and displays important features and events of the hotel.
- The tent card is a card made of glossy paper and looks like a tent and is kept on the reading table of the guest in the guestroom.
- The card elicits important information about the hotel to the in-house regarding the facilities and services of the hotel and the events taking place in the property.

GUEST ROOM KEY CONTROL

- One of reception's important jobs have been issuing room keys to the guests and them take them back for safe keeping when the guests went out.
- The keys had a large and heavy tags attached to them to stop gusts from walking off with them.
- The tags were numbered so that the keys could be hung on a ***"key rack"*** when not in use. The key rack was usually situated behind the desk.
- The old fashioned metal key was a security risk. Guests often missed or mislaid them.

- Thus the modern hotels started using electronic keys as a solution to the problem. These keys were made of plastic and punched or magnetically coded with the door code.
- These keys do not have the room number printed on them, so the guest has to be given an additional key card showing this.
- So, the guest has to keep this card separate from the electronic room key in case the latter is stolen.

MESSAGES AND MAIL HANDLING

HANDLING INCOMING MESSAGES OF GUESTS (VERBAL AS WELL AS TELEPHONE)

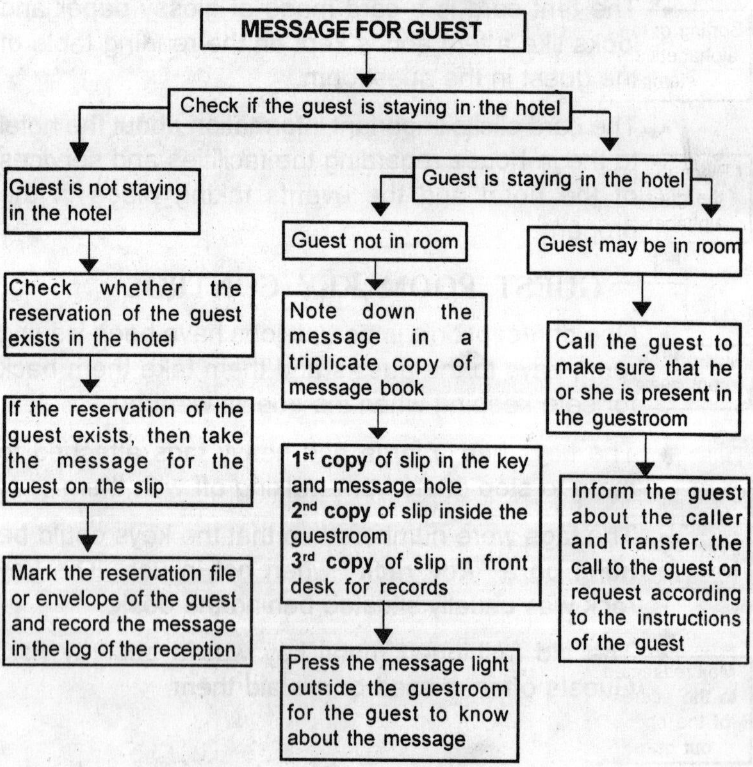

HANDLING OF MAILS AT THE INFORMATION COUNTER OF FRONT OFFICE

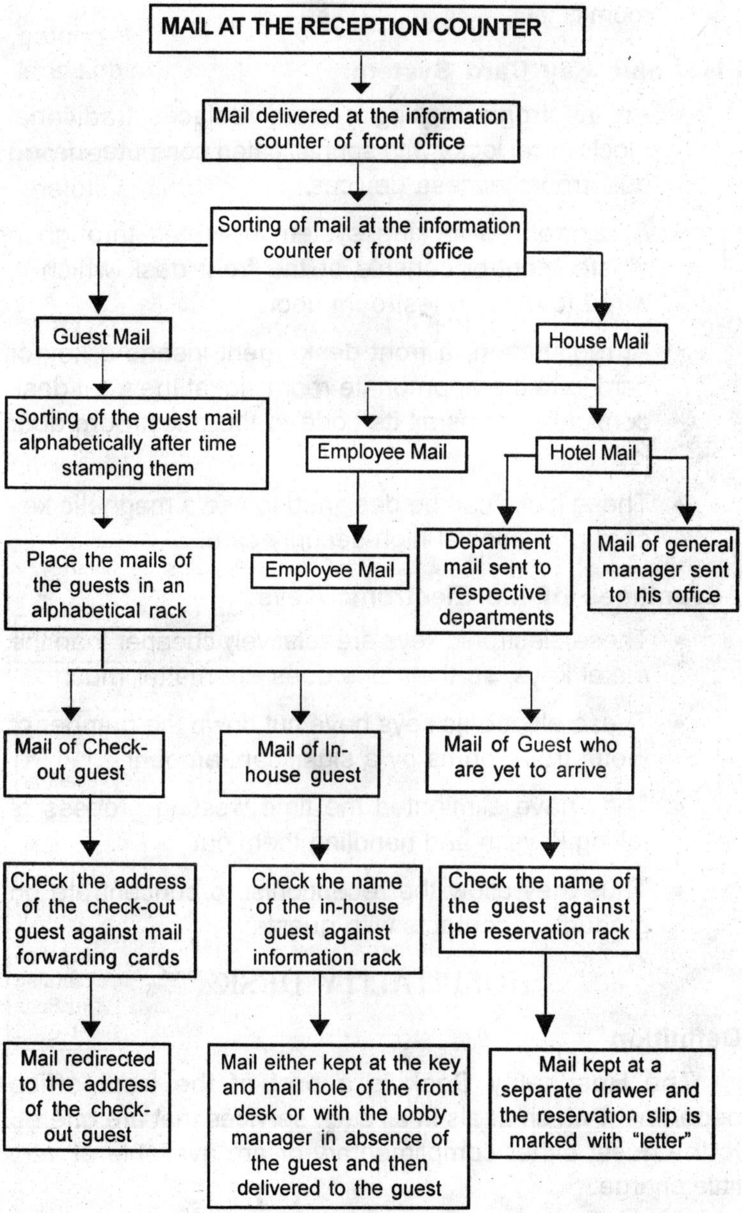

- The room lock is programmed to accept only the code on the electronic key, which is changed every time the room is let.

Electronic Key Card System:

- An electronic locking system replaces traditional mechanical locks with sophisticated computer-based guestroom access devices.
- A centralized locking system operates through a master control console at the front desk which is wired to every guestroom door.
- At registration, a front desk agent inserts a key or card in to the appropriate room slot at the front desk console to transmit its code to the guestroom door lock.
- These locks can be designed to use a magnetic key card or a special high-security card.

Advantages of the Electronic Keys:

- These electronic keys are relatively cheaper than the metal keys, so their loss does not matter much.
- These electronic keys have cut down the number of thefts from rooms by a significant amount.
- They have eliminated the time wasting process of taking keys in and handling them out.
- Thus they allow the receptionist to concentrate on productive contacts with guests.

HOSPITALITY DESK

Definition

The Hospitality Desk is a part of the front office department which deals in all such services that are offered to the guest either complimentary or are available at very little charge.

Staff

The Hospitality Desk is generally managed by the Guest Relation Executive, hostesses and airport executives.

Services Provided by the Hospitality Desk

1. *Aarti*, *Tika* and Garlanding of VVIP, VIP and foreigner guests
2. Personalized stationery
3. Flowers and fruits in the guestroom
4. Free airport pick-up and drop to the VVIP and VIP guests
5. Assistance in shopping
6. Guiding foreign guest on tours and shopping
7. Baby-sitting

Functions of the Hospitality Desk

1. Welcoming the VIP guests on arrival
2. Courtesy call to VIP guests
3. Ensuring comfortable stay for the VIP guests
4. Escorting the VIP guests to the rooms

COMPLAINTS HANDLING

Types of Complaints

a) Mechanical Complaints:

- Most guest complaints relate to the malfunction of the hotel equipments.
- This generally include problems with climate control, lighting, electricity, room furnishings, ice machines, vending machines, door keys, plumbing, television sets, elevators and so on.

b) Attitudinal Complaints:

- The guests may make attitudinal complaints when they feel insulted by rude behavior of the staffs.
- Guests who overhear staff conversations or who complaints from the hotel staff members may also express attitudinal complaints.

c) Service-related Complaints:

- Guests make service-related complaints when they experience a problem with hotel service.
- Service –related complaints may be wide-ranging and may include long waiting time for service, lack of assistance with luggage, untidy rooms, phone difficulties, missed wake-up calls, cold or ill-prepared food, or ignored request for additional supplies.

d) Unusual Complaints:

- Guests may also complaint about the absence of swimming pool, lack of transportation services and bad weather and so on.
- Hotels have little or no control over the situations involving unusual complaints.

Guidelins for Complaint Handling

- When expressing a complaint, the guest may be quite angry. Front office staff members should not go alone to a guestroom to investigate a problem or otherwise risk potential danger.
- Front office staff members should not make promises that exceed their authority.
- If a problem cannot be solved, front office staff should admit this to the guest early on. Honesty is the best policy when dealing with guest complaints.

- Front desk agents should be advised that some guests complain as part of their nature, the front office should develop an approach for dealing with such guests.

Steps to Followed in Handling Complaints

1. Avoid conflict
2. Listen to the guest patiently
3. Show sympathy towards the guest and apologize for the poor service
4. Do not justify untill and unless the situation demands
5. Ask questions to learn about the details of the complaint
6. Take action
7. Follow up with the guest after the action has been taken
8. Take feedback from the guest.

GUEST HSITORY

See Chart on next page.

- Guest History Management is a very important function of the front office department of the hotel.
- Most of the front office departments of hotels maintain records of the guests coming to the hotel which helps them to create a database of the guests and take care of the special considerations of the guests whenever they arrive the next time at the hotel.
- These records of the financial and personal information of the guests are maintained in formats which are called Guest History Cards.

GUEST HISTORY CARD

NAME:			NATIONALITY:	
ADDRESS:			DATE OF BIRTH:	
			WEDDING ANNIVERSARY:	
			ANY OTHER IMPORTANT DATE	
ARRIVAL DATE	NO. OF DAYS	ROOM NO.	PREFERENCE IF ANY	NORMALLY BOOKED THROUGH
				AGENT / CO.
				CONTACT
				NORMAL BILLING INSTRUCTIONS
			COMMENTS IF ANY:	

- The guest history cards serve as important tools of information for the front office management and help the front office to draft a profile of the guest based on his or her previous stay.
- The information in the guest history card is taken by the front office assistant at the time of reservation, registration and also at the time of the departure of the guests from the hotel.
- Thus, guest history management helps the hotel to maintain a good relationship with the guests and also helps the hotel management to get rid of unwanted guests by refusing them guestrooms.

10

ROOM SELLING TECHNIQUES

UPSELLING AT THE FRONT DESK

Defintion

Up-selling can be defined as a process of selling a higher priced commodity to a guest than that a guest had actually requested for. E.g. A front office assistant sells a suite room to a guest who had originally requested for a double room.

Brief Description

- Up-selling is a very important selling tool used by the hospitality industry sectors across the world.
- In hotels, all the revenue generating departments try to up-sell products such as accommodation product, food and beverage products and a large number of other products and services.
- Up-selling is also used widely by the front office department employees in order to get more business from the guests by recommending them to purchase a higher priced commodity.

- At front desk it is easier to up-sell to a guest coming to the hotel without any reservation.
- The receptionist should have a proper physical appearance and excellent grooming in order to create a good impression on the newly arrived guest.
- The front desk assistant should also have a very good communication skill in order to talk fluently with the guest.
- The front desk assistant should greet the guest warmly and explain the various categories of guestrooms available in the property and should highlight the expensive categories of rooms such as suites to the guests with their features.
- Thus, the front desk assistant should be able to understand the need of the guest and provide him with the best type of room available and at the same time maximize the business for the hotel.

Benefits of Up-selling

- Up-selling increases the revenue of the hotel and thus also increases the profit of the hotel.
- Up-selling enables the guests to purchase a better quality product and thus gives them an opportunity to experience and use the better quality product.
- Up-selling benefits the employees also as the front desk assistants are given rewards on the amount of up-selling they do to generate for the hotel.

DISCOUNTS

Definition

Discounts can be defined as price reduction which is offered to the guest by the hotel on various products such as rooms and food and beverage service and other accessory products and services.

The Main Reasons of Offering Discounts

1. ***To Reduce the Impact of Off Season***
   - Discounts play a major role in reducing the impact of off or low season which many hotels face.
   - Discounts assure the hotel some business by attracting guests during off season.
2. ***To Sell High Priced and Slow Moving Products Such as Suites***
   - Discounts help in the sale of high-priced products such as *suites* in hotels which are not sold very frequently and so come in the category of slow moving products.
3. ***To Build a Good Relationship With the Guest***
   - Discounts help in establishing a good relationship with the guest as price-sensitive guests are attracted by this strategy of the hotel.
4. ***To Build Repeat Business With the Guest***
   - Discounts help in generating repeat business for the hotel by attracting the guests again for the next time to come and stay with the hotel and in this way, generates revenue for the hotel.
5. ***To Compete With the Other Palyers in the Market***
   - Discounts help in keeping the prices of all the hotels in a particular market in a control manner.
   - Thus, discounts help in increase in competition with the various players and thus help a hotel to beat its competitors and be market leader.

Benefits to a Hotel for Providing Discounts to its Guests

1. Increase in customer loyalty of the hotel
2. Increase in sale of the slow moving and expensive products
3. Increase in sale during the period of off season
4. Increase in the overall revenue generation and profit of a hotel
5. Increase in popularity and gaining the position of a market leader.

11

NIGHT AUDIT IN FRONT OFFICE

NIGHT AUDIT IN FRONT OFFICE

Some Important Terms Used in the Night Audit Routine

1. Audit Trail	:	An organized flow of source documents detailing each step in the processing of a transaction.
2. Daily Transcript	:	A detailed report of all guests accounts that **indicates each charge transaction affecting a guest account for the day, used as a worksheet to** detect posting errors.
3. Supplemental Transcript	:	A detailed report of all non-guest accounts that **indicates each charge transaction that affected a non-guest account that day, used as a worksheet to detect posting errors.**
4. End-of-day	:	An arbitrary stopping point for the business day.

5. Room Status Report	:	A report that allows the front desk agent to **identify the ready rooms, typically prepared as a part of the night audit.**
6. Room Variance Report	:	A report listing any discrepancies between front **desk and housekeeping room statuses.**
7. System Update	:	A fully automated audit routine accomplishing the same functions as a non-computerised night **audit; daily system updates enable file** reorganization, system maintenance, and report production, and provide an end-of-day time frame.
8. Bucket Check	:	The night auditor's check of room rate postings on guest folios against the housekeeping department's report of occupied rooms and the front desk room rack; helps ensure that rates have been posted for all occupied rooms and helps reduce the occupancy errors caused when front desk agents do not properly complete check-in and check-out procedures.
9. In Balance	:	A term used to describe the state of accounts when the totals of debit amounts and credit amounts are equal.
10. Out-of-balance	:	A term used to describe the state of accounts when the total of debit amounts and credit amounts are not equal.

11. Control Folio : An accounting department document used internally by a front office computer to support all account postings by department during a system update routine.

12. D card : A night auditor's report used in semi-automated front office accounting systems.

THE NIGHT AUDIT AND ITS MAIN FUNCTIONS

Functions of Night Audit

- The front office must regularly review and verify the accuracy and completeness of the guest and the non-guest accounting records.
- The front office audit is a daily review of guest account transactions recorded at the front desk against revenue centre transactions.
- The routine front office audit helps to guarantee the accuracy, reliability, and the thoroughness of front office accounting.
- The front office audit is usually called the night audit because hotels generally perform the same during the late evening hours.

The Main Functions of the Night Audit

- Verification of the posted entries to the guest and non-guest accounts.
- Balancing all the front office accounts.
- Resolution of the room status discrepancies.
- Monitoring the guest credit limits.
- Production of the various operational and managerial reports.

The Role of the Night Auditor

- The night auditor should be familiar with the nature of the cash transactions affecting the front office accounting system.
- The night auditor typically tracks the room revenues, occupancy percentage, and other standard operating statistics.
- In addition, the auditor prepares a daily summary of the cash, check, and credit card activities that occurred at the front desk.
- The night auditor summarizes and reports the results of operations to front office management.

DETAILS OF THE NIGHT AUDIT PROCESS

The Time of the Night Audit

- The night auditor generally works in the night shift, from 2300 Hrs. to 0700 Hrs.
- The business day of a hotel ends with the beginning of the night audit process.
- The period in between the audit when the same is taking place is called the **Audit Work Time**.
- Generally the night audit starts at around 0100 Hrs. in most of the hotel except the casino hotels where the night audit takes place at around 0400 Hrs.

The Audit Posting Formula Used in the Front Office

Previous Balance + Debits - Credits = Net Outstanding Balance

PB DR CR NOB

THE TEN STEPS OF NIGHT AUDIT

The following are the ten steps of the night audit process in front office:

1. Completion of Outstanding Postings.
2. Reconciliation of Room Status Discrepancies.
3. Balancing All Departmental Accounts.
4. Verification of the Room Rates
5. Verification of the No-show reservations.
6. Posting Room Rates and Taxes.
7. Preparation of Required Reports.
8. Preparation of Cash Receipts for Deposit.
9. Clear or Back Up the System.
10. Distribution of the Reports.

Brief Description of the Ten Steps of the Night Audit Process

1. *Completion of Outstanding Postings:*

- One of the primary functions of the night audit is to ensure that all transactions affecting guest and non-guest accounts are posted to appropriate folios before the end of the day.
- Traditionally, the first step of the night audit is to complete all outstanding postings.
- The night auditor should therefore confirm that all transactions have been posted to the proper accounts as they are received at the front desk before starting the audit routine.
- In addition to completing the posting function, the auditor verifies that all vouchers for revenue centre transactions are posted.

- In an automated hotel, this is done by generating printed posting reports from the accounting system.
- If the figures are identical, the systems are in balance. If they are not the same, the auditor begins to compare transactions that have been omitted or improperly posted.

2. ***Reconciliation of Room Status Discrepancies:***

- Room status discrepancies should be resolved in time during the night audit process since imbalances can lead to lost business and thus cause confusion in the front office.
- Errors in room status can lead to lost and uncollectible room revenue and omissions in postings.
- The front office should maintain accurate room status information to effectively determine the number and types of rooms available for sale.
- At the end of the day, the room status report is compared with the housekeeper's report and the bucket where the registration cards for in-house guests are kept.
- In automated hotels, the checkout process is normally linked to a room management function that automatically monitors and updates the room status.
- Though the room status discrepancies are rare in automated hotels, the night audit process is still necessary to ensure accuracy.

3. ***Balancing all Departmental Accounts:***

- It is generally considered more easy for the front office staffs to balance all the departments first and then look for posting errors with-in an out-of-balance department in order to avoid discovering errors in the night audit process.

- The night auditor typically balances all the revenue centre departments using the source documents that originated in the revenue centre.
- The night auditor balances all front office transactions against the departmental transaction information.
- The process used to balance the revenue centre departments is often called the trial balance.
- The trial balance usually uncovers any corrections or adjustments that need to be made during the night audit process.
- The trial balance is performed before posting the room rates and thus, if the trial balance is correct but the final balance is wrong, then the auditor can find that the error has been made in the posting of the room rates and taxes.
- Thus, performing the trial balance before the room rates posting avoids the creation of confusion during the night audit process due to the errors.

4. ***Verification of Room Rates:***

- The night auditor has to verify the room rates properly before posting them in the guest accounts.
- The night auditor has to check that proper rates have been allotted to the guest on the basis of the plans, package, discounts etc.
- The proper use of room revenue and count information can form a solid basis for room revenue analysis.
- The night auditor is responsible for calculating the room revenue and reporting it as part of the night audit or it may be done automatically by the front office computer system.

5. ***Verifying the No-show Reservations:***

- The night auditor is responsible for clearing the reservation rack and post charges to no-show accounts.
- While posting the no-show charges, the night audit should carefully verify that the reservation was guaranteed and the guest did not register in the hotel.
- The no-show billing should be handled with great care by correctly recording the transactions.
- The night auditor should properly bill the no-show guests since incorrect billing may lead the credit card company to revaluate its legal agreement and relationship with the hotel.
- All front office staff must adhere to established no-show procedures when handling reservation cancellation or modifications.

6. ***Posting of Room Rates and Taxes:***

- The posting of room rates and taxes takes place at the end of the business day.
- Once the room rates are posted, a room rate and tax report is generated for the front office management review.
- In the automated hotels, the room rates and taxes are posted in the individual guest folios automatically at one go.
- Once the night auditor verifies the room rates and the taxes to posted, the computer automatically posts the room rates and taxes in the individual guest folios in few minutes.
- In addition, the automatic charge postings are accurate, with no chance for pick-up, tax calculation or posting errors.

- Thus, the auto-posting of room rates and taxes can save night audit time and improve accuracy in night audit.

7. ***Preparation of Reports:***

- The night auditor prepares reports that indicate the status of front office activities and operations.
- The following are the important reports generated by the night auditor during the night audit:

- *Daily Operations Report*
    - The daily operations report summarizes the day's business and provides insight into revenues, operating statistics, and cash transactions related to the front office.
    - This report is considered the most important outcome of the front office audit.
- *High Balance Report*
    - The high balance report identifies guests whose charges are approaching an account credit limit designated by the hotel.
    - In automated hotels, the high balance report may be produced at any time during the day.
- *Group Summary Report*
    - The group summary report generally details the various activities of the groups registered in the hotel.
    - It generally shows the number of rooms occupied by each group in the hotel, the number of guests for each group, and the revenue generated by each group.
- *VIPs Report*
    - The VIPs report gives information about the total number of VIP guests registered in the hotel.

- This report is useful for providing various special services to these guests and also for the hotel in its ability to draw such type of elite guests.

8. ***Deposition Of Cash:***

- The night auditor prepares a cash deposit voucher as an important part of the night audit process.
- If the front office cash receipts have not been deposited in the bank, the auditor compares the postings of cash payments and paid-outs with actual cash on hand.
- A copy of the front office cashier shift report may be included in the cash deposit envelope to support any overage, shortage, or due back balances.
- Since account and departmental balancing often involve cash transactions, accurate cash depositing may depend on an effective audit process.

9. ***Clear or Back Up the system:***

- In manual and semi-automated system of front office operations, the totals must be cleared from the system after the night audit is complete.
- Manual systems are cleared by moving the closing balance from the night audit report to the opening balance of the next day's report.
- In semi-automated systems, the totals in the account posting machine must be brought to zero balance.
- A system back-up in the night audit routine is unique to the computerised front office systems.
- Computer generated front office information should be copied onto magnetic disk depending the system configuration.
- Many computer systems have two types of system back-up.

- ***A daily back-up*** simply creates a copy of the front office electronic files on magnetic disk or tape.
- ***A weekly back-up*** which not only copies the daily information, but also eliminates account transactions information which are of no value any more.

10. *Distribution of Reports:*

- It is an essential responsibility of the night auditor to properly hand over the various reports of the night audit to the authorized and designated individuals due to the confidential nature of the reports.
- The distribution of the reports prepared is the final step of the night audit routine.
- Managerial decisions can be properly made only if the reports are properly, accurately and timely completed.

THE VARIOUS TYPES OF ERRORS IN THE NIGHT AUDIT

- Numerous types of errors occurred in the various transactions of the front office can be easily identified during the night audit process.
- These errors mostly occur due to faulty posting and clerical operation.
- The following are some of the common errors made in the front office:
- **Pickup Errors:**
  - This type of error is common in the manual and the semi-automated front office systems.
  - This type of error occurs when a previous closing balance of a particular day have been wrongly written as the opening balance of the next day.

- Thus the resulting closing balance of the following day will also become incorrect.
- Thus, the front office cashier should properly access the previous balance of an account folio, post the debits and credits, and calculate a new current balance.

- **Transposition Errors:**
    - This type of error is also common in the manual and the semi-automated front office systems.
    - This type of error occurs when numbers related to a transaction are reversed. (***For instance, writing or entering $523 instead of $532 in the account posting machine.***)
    - A transposition error can usually be identified by subtracting the smaller number from the larger number and dividing the result by 9. If the result is a whole number, then the problem is mostly likely to be a transposition error.

- **Missing Folios:**
    - This type of error is also common in the semi and non-automated front office systems.
    - Due to the incorrect filing of the folios or removal of the same from the folio bucket, often the front office systems become out of balance.
    - This normally occurs when the front office cashier forgetfully allows the guest folio to remain behind the room tab instead of bringing the same to the front of the room tab after the departure of the guest.
    - Folios can also seem to misplace if the front office cashier of a particular shift forgets to inform the front office cashier of the next shift that the

same has been sent to the credit manager for his review.

- Thus, the front office cashier should handle the guest folios with great care to avoid the inconvenience caused by missing the same.

12

HOSPITALITY

HOSPITALITY AND ITS DELIVERY

Concept of Hospitality

- The concept of hospitality is the generous and cordial provision of services to the guests arriving at the various hospitality properties.
- These services, in the hotel industry, can include room accommodations, food and beverages, meeting facilities, reservations, information on hotel services, information on local attractions and so on.
- Hospitality is very subjective concept, and the degree of hospitality a guest perceives has implications for the overall final success of the hotel.
- Thus it is responsibility of the future professionals of the hospitality industry should develop a strong sense of responsibility for providing professional hospitality.
- Thus the delivery of hospitality efficiently to the guests is an essential responsibility of the hospitality professionals in order to satisfy the guests to the utmost extent.

Importance of Hospitality

- Hospitality is very important consideration for both the guest and the hotel entrepreneur.
- Every guest expects and deserves hospitable treatment. Providing hospitality to meet guests' needs involves not only a positive attitude but a range of services that make the stay of the guest comfortable as well as enjoyable.
- If the market being served by the hotel is composed of business travellers, a hotel staff will find that their needs revolve around schedules and flexible delivery of hotel services.
- Thus the hotel restaurant must be well organized to be able to provide healthy and quick breakfast. The hotel should offer services such as wake-up call, advanced telephone systems, fax facilities and computers. Besides, the hotel should also be able to arrange for the conference and meeting facilities.
- The success or failure in providing hospitality often determines the success or failure of the hotel. Thus capitalizing on opportunities to provide hospitality is essential. The failure to make the most of these changes directly affects the hotel's financial success.
- The hospitality deliverers know it very well that the guest who is not treated with hospitality will choose to do business with a competitor and may also influence others not to try the particular hotel.
- The entrepreneur who is aware of the competition realizes that negative advertising will severely affect the profit-and-loss statement.
- Thus hospitable treatment of guest must be more than just an option; it must be standard operating procedure. It is a concept that must be adopted as a corporate tenet and organized for effective delivery.

Managing the Delivery of Hospitality

- It is not enough for the front office manager to decide that the members of the front office staff should provide good service and display hospitality to the guests.
- To provide satisfactory hospitality to all guests at all times, front office managers must develop and administer a service management program, which highlights a company's focus on meeting customers' needs and allows a hotel to achieve its financial goals.
- The management must work with full efforts behind the scene to develop a plan to ensure that the front office staffs deliver hospitality with a professional attitude.
- For example, management may decide to implement one or two specific, immediate changes on learning that a guest's needs have been overlooked.
- Thus the management should try to develop a program aimed at meeting the needs of a hotel's prime market – guests who continue to do business with the hotel – provides the foundation for long-term successful delivery of hospitality.
- Management's commitment to a service management program must be an integral to organization as effective market planning, cost-control programs, budgeting and human resource management.
- Thus service management program is the most visible responsibility because it affects all other objectives of the hotel.
- Service management ensures that there is a commitment to a long-range effort by appointing

someone within the organization to be responsible for developing, organizing, and delivering it.

- The owner and general manager must make financial commitment to ensure the success of the program.
- An important component of the program is motivating employees to deliver hospitality on a continual basis through incentive programs.
- The goal of any lodging organization should be to extend the same degree of hospitality to guest who arrives on a busy day and also to a guest who arrives on a slag day.

SERVICE MANAGEMENT

The Service Strategy Statement

- To produce an effective service management program, management must devise a service strategy statement, a formal recognition by management that the hotel will strive to deliver the products and services desired by the guest in a professional manner.
- Hence to accomplish this, the management must first identify the guest's needs.
- The staffs working at the entry-level position in a hotel are in direct contact with the guest and so they can anticipate the needs and demands of the guests in a better way.
- Thus the hotel management should use the observations of the entry-level position employees as a baseline for beginning to understand guests' needs while they are away from home, and thus the hotel management would be able to satisfy the guests in a better way.

- Thus, in addition to identifying generally what guests want, management should survey guests about the particular property to determine what services they expect and how they want these services to be delivered.
- The general manager may assign this task to the marketing and sales director, who may start reviewing and summarizing customer comment cards, which are usually held on file for six months to one year.
- A review of the areas in which the hotel has disappointed its guests, will provide a basis for determining where to begin a guest survey.
- The problem areas identified from this study are then used as the focus of a simple survey from.
- The survey may be administered by a member of the marketing and sales department at various times during the day.
- This information, as well as that collected from the comment cards, will give a general indication of what guest wants.

Developing the Service Strategy Statement

Once the management has identified what guests want, it can develop a service strategy statement. The statement should include: -

- A commitment to make service from top-level ownership and management a top priority in the company.
- A commitment to develop and administer a service management program.
- A commitment to train employees to deliver service efficiently.

- A commitment of financial resources to develop incentives for the employees delivers the services who deliver the services.

These directives will serve as guidelines in the development of a service management program. More important, they force management to think of service as a long-range effort.

Here is one example of a service strategy statement: -

The owners of The Times Hotel, management, and staff will combine forces to establish a Service to Our Guests program, administered by management and delivered by staff. Delivery of service to our guests is crucial to the economic viability of our hotel. The owners of the hotel will provide financial support to the people who deliver hospitality on a daily basis.

Moments of Truth in Hotel Service Management

- Central to the development of a guest service program is the management of "moments of truth", a circumstance in which a guest comes into contact with any aspect of the company, however remote, and thereby has an opportunity to form an impression.
- Every time the guest comes in contact with some aspect of the hotel, he or she judges its hospitality.
- Guests who are told by reservationists that they must "take his room at his rate or stay elsewhere" will not feel that hospitality is the primary consideration at the particular hotel.
- The guest who is crammed into an elevator with half the housekeeping crew, their vacuum cleaners, and bins of soiled laundry will not feel welcomed. All these impressions make the guest feel that service at the particular is mismanaged.

- Whether a guest considers an event a moment of truth or barely notices, it is a cumulative review of the delivery of hospitality.
- Thus if the guest is to appreciate the service of a particular property, it is essential that these moments of truth be well managed. This challenge is not to be viewed as mission impossible but rather as an organized and concerned effort by owners, management, and employees.

Employee buy-in Concept

- All the sophisticated marketing programs, well organized sales promotions, outstanding architectural designs, and certified management staffs form only the backdrop for the delivery of hospitality.
- The frontline employee is the link in the service management program. He or she must deliver the service with a high level of consistency in order to satisfy the guest to the utmost extent.
- To have a high standard of service, it is necessary to create and maintain a motivating environment in which service people can find personal reasons for giving their best to the employees.
- Thus a consistent high level of service will be provided only by employees who are committed to the service management program.
- The hotel management has an important to play in order to foster this commitment in the employees.
- The following are some of the strategies that can adopted to motivate the staffs of a hotel: -
    a) Financial incentive programs should be implemented in order to motivate the staffs to give production.

b) Employee stock ownership programs also provide an incentive for employees to realize financially the importance of delivering a consistently high level of hospitality.

c) Other reward systems may include preferential treatment in scheduling shifts, longer vacations, and extra vacations, and extra holidays.

d) Long range rewards may include promotion opportunities.

Screening Employees who Deliver Hospitality

- It is an important job of the management to decide the employee character traits needed to provide hospitality while developing a service management program.
- When evaluating the candidates for the frontline service positions, interviews should be structured to screen out employees who are not able to deal with the demands of the guest service.
- Group discussions among the managerial staff will help to highlight the attributes of a person who will be able to deliver hospitality.
- These discussions should lead to a rather informal procedure for screening employees.
- Questions which determine whether candidates display maturity and self-esteem are clear, possess social graces and have a high level of tolerance for continued guest contact.
- The managers who are ware of what they are looking for in employees are better able to secure the right people for the right jobs.

Training for Hospitality Management

- Part of the service management program involves employee training to deliver hospitality.
- Just as managers discuss what they want in an employee, managers decide what must be done to convey hospitality to travellers who are away from home.
- This decision regarding this aspect is taken after performing a discussion and gathering valuable inputs from other employee.
- Using the guest cycle, the planning group determines what each frontline employee must do at each point to extend hospitality.
- It is extremely important to take care that the communications of hospitality must be identified, so that each employee can be properly trained to convey them.
- The key to make training program successful is to know what the management wants from the trainees to be able to do after the completion of the training program.
- An effective training process starts with performance analysis.
- The management must analyze the various jobs to be done in serving the customer well, and then spell out the knowledge, attitudes, and skills required of the person doing the jobs.

Evaluating the Service Management Program

- All programs require methods for evaluating whether the program has successfully its achieved goal or not.

- Hence, as a step towards this direction, the hotel managements have developed a sound evaluation procedure on identifying the guest's moments of truth.
- The more research put into identifying the components of the guest service cycle for a specified hotel property.
- Specific desired behaviors of the guest as well as the employee can be observed and measured.
- Customer comment card is an important evaluation tool for the hotel as the hotel management comes to know the about the performance of the various operational departments of the hotel through the comments of the guests.
- Owners, managers, and employees who are committed to the service management program develop additional programs for determining the satisfaction level of the guests. One another method that can be used to obtain useful feedback from the guests is by having frontline staff, such as desk clerk, inquire about the guests' visit during check-out.
- A method of communicating the responses of the guests to the appropriate departments, which can rectify the errors or reward the frontline employee, will complete the process of evaluating the success of a service management program.

Follow Through

- Vital to any service management program is the continued implementation of the program over time.
- In the hospitality industry, continued implementation of the program over time can very difficult.

- A hotel operates throughout the year and a large number of jobs are involved and performed in keeping it running smoothly and profitably.
- Management can begin a service management program with the best of its intentions, but too often it is dropped due to the day-to-day work operation pressures.
- The difference between a program and continuous commitment is management. Management is the key to implementing an effective guest service program.
- The commitment to hospitality is not a casual one; it requires constant attention, research, training and evaluation.
- Only with this commitment can a hotel ensure hospitality everyday for every guest.

13

COMPUTERS IN HOSPITALITY

COMPUTERS IN HOSPITALITY

Technology has become the basic requirement in the hospitality industry in the 21st century.

Hence every professional in the hospitality industry agrees on its increasing importance for the welfare and comfort of the guests primarily and then the employees at large and thus generating long run benefits, profits and goodwill at large.

Today, the hospitality industry is slowly being transformed through the application of advanced technological innovation, and this transformation is something more radical than mere improvements in machines.

Today, Information Technology or IT has become the essence of the hospitality industry.

Information Technology is usually associated with the electronic storage and retrieval of information the various operations of an organization

Hospitality operatives are increasingly finding that new systems give them more skill, interest , responsibility and control over how they perform their jobs.

The organizations vision of a successful implementation of information technology can thus have a positive impact on the way in which managers perceive their role.

Thus, in the battle of hospitality entrepreneur against fate i.e. customer demand, his or her skills and techniques are like weapons, that they can use in a variety of way out of which information technology is just are of these weapons which becomes extremely important in the drive for a successful and profit maximizing establishment.

Car Rental

- Car rental is a flourishing business throughout the world and is complementing the hotel industry by meeting the requirements of the guests demanding car rental during their arrival, stay and departure from the hotel.
- The car rental has also become a business in the metropolitan and other important cities of India.
- The important target markets for the car rental business are tourists, hotel guests as well as business and corporate travellers while traveling to other cities and countries.
- Nowadays, computers have fully automated the operations of the car rental services around many countries of the world.
- In the continents of Europe and America, the Information and Reservation systems such as **Amadeus**, **Sabre** and **Galileo** are used for car rental and information.
- The world's largest car rental company Hutch has also developed its own Information and Reservation system for providing car rental services to their potential clients.

- In India, the car rental service is at bud stage with a very few companies having fully automated car rental operations.
- ***Wheels*** is one of the frontline company in India solely dealing with the rental of vehicles and thus fulfilling care rental requirements for the tourists, guests and other business travellers.
- TCI, Thomas Cook, Graha Tours and Travels and other travel and tour operating agencies have transport divisions which are companies dealing with car rental services.

  The international Information and Reservation System such as Amadeus, Sabre and Galileo enables the instant confirmation of the car rental services in case of international booking through the computerized system.
- The computerized car rental services operating in a city domestically can have instant access about the free cars and taxis very quickly through their computerized network.
- The computerized car rental service companies maintain and updated inventory of all the available cars for rent and thus traces all the free cars and sends them for services to the customers efficiently and promptly.
- When international bookings are accepted by the IRS or travel agents, the bookings are routed to the sister concerns of the travel agencies through telephone, fax, e-mail etc. and thus the sister concern travel agencies in the host country receives international business and earns profit.

Airlines Operations

- The airlines industry has the maximum amount of the computerization in comparison to any other industry in the travel and tourism segment.
- The airlines industry uses the Global Distribution System to book air tickets for the various airline companies operating around the world.
- The Global Distribution system helps in achieving a better occupancy percentage in the flights and thus also plays a vital role in the marketing and popularity of the airline companies.
  - The first Information and Reservation System was developed in the country of U.S.A in the year 1970.
  - The IRS provided total information about the travel and tourism industry and also provided vital information about the airline industry.
  - The IRS also provided the facility of central reservation system for booking of the airline tickets in the flights of the various airline companies operating in U.S.A.

Adavantages of IRS

- The IRS provided information about the flight schedules, flight timings, flight availability and also provided booking facility through the central reservation system.
- The IRS helps the airline companies to market and distribute their products to the target market and thus improve their efficiency and improve their market image.
- The IRS helps the travel agents to disseminate information travel segments and their demands,

details of the flight schedules and bookings of airlines.

- The IRS also helps the various tour operators and departments of tourism of the various countries to gain information about making their services efficient and understand the customers and their requirements in better way.
- Many IRS are now providing information and reservation in various other product lines such as hotel, cruises, tours, car rentals and so on.

- AMADEUS is a very popular Information and Reservation System founded in the year in 1987 by airline companies: Air France, Lufthansa, Iberia and SAS of which SAS has withdrawn its share holds.
- AMADEUS is now known as the AMADEUS Global Distribution System and is electronic information and booking system providing worldwide distribution of the airline reservation.
- AMADEUS displays flight information about 700 airline companies and accepts bookings for 430 airline companies.
- AMADEUS now provides information and reservation facilities about accommodation in various world class hotels and car rental companies around the globe and also provides information about Rails, Tours and Cruises and their reservations.
- AMADEUS has established more than 50 companies around the globe in partnership with the various domestic companies of the different countries.
- These domestic companies are also called the National Marketing Companies of AMADEUS and these companies help to market the products of AMADEUS along with active customer service.

- GALILEO is also an important Information and Reservation System which was commissioned in the year 1987 in England and was a joint venture of many airline companies.
- GALILEO was started with the purpose of providing information to the travel agents about the various airline companies and their reservation through the central reservation system.
- GALILEO also has collaboration with various domestic companies of different countries to distribute and sell their products to the customers and also provides information and reservations for hotels, cars, tours etc.
- SABRE opened in joint venture is perhaps the largest and most popular Information and Reservation System of U.S.A.
- SABRE provides central reservation system facility for airlines, hotels and car rental in the country of U.S.A but was not too much successful in Europe.

Services of Computers in the Hotel Industry

Reservation

1) The computes are widely used in the reservation sectionof the front office departments of fully automated hotels around the world.
2) In, India also, in most of the well-known properties, the room reservation system has been fully automated through the use of computers.
3) Computers have replaced the traditional Whitney system of reservation which used to generate a lot of paperwork.
4) The computers used in the reservation sections maintain an updated inventory of the available rooms of the property for reservation.

5) The computers use various packages such as FIDELIO and SHAWMANN for the processing and storage of various important guest data regarding reservations.

6) The computers can be programmed to maintain an accurate data base for the various reservation requests of the guests and thus can store them for future retrieval

7) The introduction on the Local Area Network and Wide Area Network have led to the invent of central reservation system which is a reservation network of computers of a large number of hotels.

8) Thus, many chain hotels have their own central reservation system called the CRS which enables the guests to making room reservations for a hotel in one city from another city through the city booking offices of the hotel chain.

9) Many hotels have connected their central reservation system through the airline terminal to the Information and Reservation System (Global Distribution System) which provides them with worldwide bookings.

10) Thus , the main advantage of the computerized reservation system is that, one can have an accurate record of all the dates when rooms are available for sale and one can also keep a record of all the unsold and sold rooms of the hotel for a particular date.

Food and Beverage Service

1) Computers are also widely used in the food and beverage service departments of large hotels for the smooth operation of the food and beverage service operations.

2) The computers are widely used in the preparation of guest bills for settlement and record, menu card

preparation, inventory management and a variety of other food and beverage management functions.

3) Like room reservation, the computers are also used in the reservation or restaurant table for guests to have their meals and enjoy the dining experience in the food and beverage outlets.

4) The room service section of the food and beverage department also uses computers for keeping a track on the services. The room service order-taker takes down the order of the guest through telephone and then feeds the information in the computer which is connected to a printer or a monitor in the kitchen which instantaneously displays the order and thus the order is placed.

5) The food and beverage outlets use a Point-of-Sale software for the management of the entire operations of the outlets. The following are the main functional and vital files with the help of which the outlets work:

   a) Menu File: The menu file records all thedishes in the menu of the outlet and gives a short description of them with their prices and taxes applicable.

   b) Guest Receipt: The guest receipt is an open data file and contains the guest names and items ordered by the guests. Each receipt will contain information about the guest name, name of the food and beverage outlet, the menu items ordered, individual price of the item, sub-total, taxes applicable and grand total.

c) Master File: The master file will have important details about the employees of the Food and beverage outlet: the working hours of the employees, the amount of work performed by each employee and the wages earned by the employee.

d) Inventory File: The inventory file keeps a record of all the important products required For the operation of a food and beverage outlet and thus keeps a track on the purchase and utilization of the products.

6) The computers can also be used in the preparation of the various restaurant management reports which are used for reviewing the sale of the restaurant and thus they provide an insight to the eating trends and preferences of the guests, demands of the customers and also helps to predict the future manpower requirements of a restaurant.

ACCOUNTING AND BILLING

1) Computers are also used in the accounting of rooms, room services and restaurant services and also in other departments of the hotel.

2) The computers are used for storing the rates of the various rooms in the front office which are displayed when required.

3) The computers are also used to record the various charges which are incurred by the guests during the stay in the hotel.

4) The charges are posted in the guest folio and the folios are presented to the guests at the time of departure of the guest.

5) The computers are also used in the generation of various reports in the night audit process which is conducted in the front office regularly.

BIBLIOGRAPHY

TEXT BOOK REFERENCING

1. Abbot, P. *Front Office: Procedures, Special Skills and Management*, Oxford : Butterworth-Heinemann, 1991.
2. Arthur,R., and D. Gladwell. *The Hotel Assistant Manager*. 3rd ed. London: Barrie & Rockliff, 1975.
3. Baird, C., and L. Carla. *Front Office Assignments*. London: Cassell, 1992.
4. Bardi, James A. *Hotel Front Office Management*. New York: Van Nostrand Reinhold, 1990.
5. Bardi, J.A. Hotel Front Office Management . New Jersey: John Wiley & Sons, 2003.
6. Boomer, Lucius. *Hotel Management*. New York: Harper & Row, 1938.
7. Braham, Bruce. *Computer Systems in Hotel and Catering Industry*. London: Cassell Educational Ltd., 1988.
8. Borsenik, Frank. *The Management of Maintenance and Engineering in the Hospitality Industry*. 3rd ed. New York: John Wiley & Sons, 1992.
9. Browning, Marjorie. *Night Audit Procedure*. Columbus: The Christopher Inn, March 1, 1969.
10. Burstein, Harvey. *Hotel Security Management*. New York: Praeger Publishers, 1975.

11. Buzby, Walter J. *Hotel and Motel Security Management*. Los Angeles: Security World Publishing Co., 1976.

12. Chandler, Raymond. *Trouble Is My Business*. New York: Ballantine Books, 1972.

13. Collins, Galen. *Hospitality Information Technology: Learning How to Use It*. Dubuque, IA: Hunt Publishing, 1992.

14. Dukas Peter. *Hotel Front Office Management and Operations*. 3rd ed. Dubuque, IA: Wm. C. Brown, 1970.

15. Foster, Dennis. *Rooms at the Inn: Front Office Operations and Administration*. Lake Forest, IL: Glencoe, 1992.

16. *Front Office and Reservations*. Burlingame, CA: Hyatt Corporation, 1978.

17. Gomes, Albert j. *Hospitality in Transition*. Houston: Pannell Kerr Forster, 1985.

18. Kasavana, Michael L. and Richard M. Brooks. *Managing Front Office Operations*. EI of AH&LA, 2001.

19. Kasavana, Michael L. and Richard M. Brooks. *Managing Front Office Operations*. EI of AH&LA, 2002.

20. Kasavana, Michael L. and Richard M. Brooks. *Managing Computers in the Hospitality Industry*. 2nd ed.EI of AH&LA, 1992.

21. Lundberg, Donald. *The Hotel and Restaurant Business*. 5th ed. New York: Van Nostrand Reinhold, 1989.

22. Orkin, E. Boosting Your Bottom Line with Yield Management, Cornell Hotel and Restaurant

Administration Quarterly 30, no. 3(November 1989)

23. *Property Management and Point of Sale Systems: Guide to Selection*. New York. EI of AH&LA (date unknown)
24. Rutherford, Denney G. *Hotel Management and Operations*. New York: Van Nostrand Reinhold, 1989.
25. *Starting and Managing a Small Motel*. Small Business Administration, Washington D.C.
26. *The State of Technology in the Lodging Industry*. New York. EI of AH&LA, 1980.
27. Troy, *Keys to Security*.
28. *Yield Management Systems*, (YMSI, L.C.C.), Chicago, U.S.A.
29. Vallen, G.K. & Vallen, J.J. *Check-in Check-out*. Prentice-Hall, New Jersey, U.S.A, 1996.
30. Vallen, G.K. & Abbey, J.A. *The Art and Science of Hospitality Management*. EI of AH&LA, 1987.

ELECTRONIC REFERENCING

1. http: // www.acfchefs.org
2. http: // www.ahma.com
3. http: // www.astanet.com
4. http: // www.csshotelssystems.com
5. http: // www.cssmain.com
6. http: // www.ei-ahla.org
7. http: // www.executech.com
8. http: // www.fhrai.com
9. http: // www.hitecshow.org
10. http: // www.hitis.com
11. http: //www.hospitalitynet.nl.com

12. http: // www.hostgroup.com
13. http: // www.hotelchoice.com
14. http: // www.hrnai.com
15. http: // www.invest.com
16. http: // www.lodgingsystems.com
17. http: // www.micros.com
18. http: // www.newsoft.com
19. http: // www.penton.com
20. http: // www.resortdata.com